W9-AOQ-457

The Little Book
of
BAD
TASTE

The Little Book
of

BAD
TASTE

by

KARL SHAW

BARNES
&NOBLE
BOOKS
NEW YORK

This edition published by Barnes & Noble Inc.,
by arrangement with Parragon

2002 Barnes & Noble Books
M 10 9 8 7 6 5 4 3 2 1

Produced by Magpie Books, an imprint of
Robinson Publishing Ltd, London

Copyright © Karl Shaw 1998
A special selection from *The Mammoth Book of Tasteless Lists*,
published by Robinson Publishing 1998

Cover by Design Revolution

ISBN 0-7607-3777-0

Printed in China

Contents

Introduction

"Good taste and humour are a contradiction in terms, like a chaste whore."
Malcolm Muggeridge (1903–90)

"Comedy equals tragedy plus timing."
Anon

Bad taste is wonderful. Where would good taste be without it? The Little Book of Bad Taste lap dances where other trivia books fear to tread … a celebration of life's cultural underbelly, a compendium of moving, deliciously wicked and crucially indelicate facts, plucked, dredged and squeezed from the slough of human experience. Enjoy dipping into this literary fondue of malodorous, unsavory and unappetising information, and gorge on a banquet of grisly, gruesome but true anecdotes that will amaze and disgust your friends and break the ice at dinner parties.

The following is dedicated to the heroes and heroines of bad taste, including E. Mackerchar, author of The Romance of Leprosy; *to the poet Dante Gabriel Rossetti, who had his late wife exhumed after seven years so that he could recover an unpublished manuscript; to Gina Lalopola, the Italian stripper found deceased inside the birthday cake she was supposed to leap from at a bachelor party; to the murderer of puns and of a New York policeman, George Appel, who observed as he was being strapped into the electric chair, "pretty soon you're going to see a baked Appel"; and to the late Lord Erskine of Rerrick, who bequeathed his testicles to the Bank of Scotland because it had "no balls."*

Bon appetit.

Chapter 1

ENTRÉE

10 Surprise Fillings

~

1. An Italian stripper, Gina Lalapola, was found dead inside a cake she was supposed to leap from at a bachelor party in Cosenza in 1995. She had lain suffocated inside the sealed wooden cake for more than an hour before her death was discovered.

2. The Sex Pistols guitarist Steve Jones once admitted ejaculating into a French bread roll and feeding it to fellow band member Glen Matlock as elevenses.

3. In August 1983 *The Times* reported that a man living in West Germany had found a human finger in his bread finger-roll.

4. Ursula Beckley of Long Island, USA, filed a $3.6 million suit for damages against a local supermarket in 1989 after the three-egg omelette she was making suddenly yielded an unexpected protein bonus in the form of a healthy, six-inch black snake. Her lawyers said

she was so deeply traumatized that it was unlikely that she would ever be able to look at another egg again.

5. In 1997 a couple from Carlisle, Craig Wilde and Simone Rooney, found a a six-inch bloodstained hypodermic needle inside a half-eaten loaf purchased from a local supermarket.

6. In March 1992 an American bread company was taken to court after a woman in Los Angeles found a used condom in a large loaf. In 1997 Dalvin Stokes sued the Morrison's cafeteria in Winter Haven, Florida, when he discovered a condom in his sweet potato pie. In 1997 Jeff Bolling of Hoover, Alabama, sued a McDonald's drive-in restaurant after biting into what he thought was a pickle, but which was in fact a rolled-up condom.

7. In 1991 Wang Guang, owner of the White Temple Restaurant in China, built up a huge following for his heavily spiced Sichuan-style dumplings, which were stuffed with human flesh. Over a four-year period the exotic fillings were

supplied by Guang's brother, who worked as an assistant in the local crematorium. The grim secret ingredient of the White Temple Restaurant's menu was exposed after police were tipped off by the parents of a young girl who had died in a road accident. When they came to cremate her body they discovered that parts of it were missing.

8. Although it is widely held that modern food is "less natural" than it used to be, meal-times in the nineteenth century were a far riskier activity. Business morals in the British catering industry were never lower than in Queen Victoria's day. Deliberate food adulteration, with no laws to prevent it, grew to horrific proportions as food suppliers cheerfully ripped off and poisoned their customers at the same time. Some of the most common frauds included the use of ground Derbyshire stone instead of flour, fake Gloucester cheese colored with red lead, baked horse offal from the knacker's yard in coffee, lead chromate in mustard and even iron bars baked in loaves to make weight. People died after eating green blancmange colored with copper

sulphate and yellow Bath buns colored with arsenic. Fifteen people died after buying sweets from a Bradford market which were found to be laced with white arsenic. Beer-drinking was possibly the most dangerous activity of all: in one year there were over 100 breweries convicted for contaminating beer with poisonous substances, including sulphuric acid, which was added to "harden" new beer, and iron sulphate, added to give it a good frothy head.

9. A recipe once favored by Indian princes involved the following: take one sparrow and stuff it inside a quail. Stuff the quail into a sand grouse, and the sand grouse inside a chicken. Stuff the chicken inside a peacock, the peacock inside a goat, and the goat inside a whole camel. Place the camel in a hole in the ground, then steam.

10. A unique case of food contamination occurred in October 1992, when nine people complained that Linda McCartney's famous brand of vegetarian pies had been spiked with steak and kidney.

The Dog's Bollocks and other Hors d'Oeuvres:
10 National Delicacies

~

1. Cena Molida – contains roasted mashed cockroaches (Belize).

2. Fried, roasted or boiled guinea pig (Ecuador).

3. Rat meat sausages (Philippines).

4. Crispy fried rat with lemon/boiled bamboo rat/desiccated petrified deer's penis (China).

5. Boodog – goat broiled inside a bag made from the carefully cut and tied goatskin. The goat is either barbecued over an open fire or cooked with a blow torch (Mongolia).

6. Fruit bat soup (Thailand).

7. Pickled puffin (North Wales, nineteenth century).

8. Larks' tongues (England, sixteenth century).

9. Lumbuli – small roast animal testicles (Ancient Rome).

10. Khachapuri – traditional cheese pie of the former Soviet Republic of Georgia. In 1995 authorities closed down a bakery whose speciality was khachapuri when it emerged that the pies were being baked in the Tbilisi morgue.

10 People who Choked to Death

1. Roman Emperor Claudius choked to death on the feather he used to tickle his gullet and induce vomiting at a banquet.

2. Pope Adrian IV, a.k.a. Nicholas Breakspear, the only English pope, choked to death when he accidentally swallowed a fly.

3. Janis Joplin, US rock singer, choked on her own vomit.

4. Sherwood Anderson, US novelist, choked to death on a toothpick.

5. Jimi Hendrix, rock guitarist, choked on his own vomit.

6. Mama Cass Elliott, obese lead singer with 1960s US band The Mamas and the Papas, choked on a chicken sandwich.

7. Jim Morrison, lead singer of The Doors, choked on his own vomit.

8. Roman Novarro, Hollywood actor, choked to death on a lead Art Deco dildo, which was thrust down his throat by two burglars. The dildo had been a present from Rudolph Valentino.

9. John "Bonzo" Bonham, Led Zeppelin drummer, choked on his own vomit.

10. Robert Pueblo, a 32-year-old from St Louis, US, stole a hot dog from a convenience store in October 1994 and crammed it into his mouth before running off. Police found him lying dead a block away with a six-inch piece of hot dog lodged in his throat.

10 Acts of Cannibalism

1. Fritz Haarmann, a meat dealer in post-World War I Germany, was the most prolific homicidal cannibal of all time. In the 1920s the "Vampire of Hanover" picked up young male refugees at the local railway station and lured them back to his ghetto apartment, where he sexually assaulted them and killed them by biting their throats. After selling their clothes and valuables he disposed of his victims by throwing the bones into the River Leine. He sold their flesh as horse meat in an open market to Hanover's mostly starving population, eating what he couldn't sell. His activities came to an end in 1924 when some young boys fishing in the river discovered several human skulls. It was estimated that Haarmann averaged two victims per week. He was only ever charged and convicted with the murders of 27 young men, aged between 13 and 20, although police estimates of the actual death toll ranged as high as 600 in one year alone. Haarmann was beheaded in Hanover prison on 15 April 1925.

2. Ed Gein, a middle-aged man from Wisconsin, was the inspiration for the film *Psycho* and later *Silence of the Lambs*. Gein was both cannibal and necrophiliac. He began by digging up female corpses to satisfy his perversions, then graduated to murder as a means of obtaining bodies. A police raid on Gein's well-stocked fridge in 1957 helped account for 15 bodies. There they discovered human skin bracelets, a human drumskin, two lips on a string, four noses in a cup and dozens of human organs. Gein later admitted that he enjoyed draping himself in the skin of his dead victims.

3. During the third crusade King Richard I dined on curried head of Saracen.

4. Lewis Keseberg was one of 87 men, women and children who set out in 1846 on a disastrous 2,000-mile trek west to California. The expedition, led by Illinois farmer George Donner and his family, was badly planned, without even enough food to survive the harsh winter. Of the original party only 47 made it to the end of the trail – and they had survived only

by eating their dead companions. Some of the survivors struck a less than penitent attitude about their terrible dilemma. Lewis Keseberg cheerfully confessed to a preference for human liver, lights and brain soup, and paid this emotional tribute to George Donner's wife Tamsen: "She was the healthiest woman I ever ate." Years later Keseberg became wealthy by opening a steakhouse.

5. American grandfather Albert Fish went to the electric chair at Sing Sing prison in 1936 after killing and eating at least 15 children. Fish wrote to the mother of his final victim, a 10-year-old girl, six years after she had vanished: "Grace sat on my lap and kissed me. I made up my mind to eat her."

6. The Milwaukee cannibal Jeffrey Dahmer admitted at his trial in February 1992 to killing and eating 17 people. Police raiding his apartment found severed heads in the fridge, skulls in his filing cabinet and body parts in a kettle. When they discovered a human heart in

the deep freeze, Dahmer explained, "I was saving it for later."

7. In 1989 the American killer/cannibal John Weber was convicted for the murder of a 17-year-old Wisconsin schoolgirl. During his trial Weber confessed that he made a pâté from the girl's leg.

8. Uganda's former President Idi Amin was a member of the Kakua tribe, who believed that if you killed a man and then ate a part of him, he would not return to haunt the murderer. In 1973 Amin ordered the assassination of his foreign minister, Michael Ondanga. Before Ondanga's body was dumped in the river, in accordance with tribal ritual, Amin removed and ate part of his liver.

9. During China's cultural revolution in the sixties and seventies, members of Mao Tse-Tung's Red Guard ate the flesh of their enemies to prove to their venerable leader that they were fully class-conscious.

10. In 1977 US government officials staged a grand opening ceremony of their brand new Department of Agriculture staff canteen, attended by Robert Bergland, US agriculture secretary. Mr Bergland unveiled a brass plaque naming it the "Alfred Packer Memorial Dining Facility," after one of America's most famous nineteenth-century frontiersmen. A few months later the plaque was hurriedly removed when someone remembered what the late Mr Packer had been chiefly famous for: he was a cannibal, convicted of killing and eating five Colorado gold prospectors in the 1870s.

10 Strange Diets

~

1. The mad Victorian artist Richard Dadd (1817–86) lived for several years exclusively on hard boiled eggs and ale.

2. In order to demonstrate the cultural inferiority of the United States, ex-Pogues lead singer Shane MacGowan once ate a Beach Boys album.

3. During the Crimean War, British soldiers were supplied with a daily ration of caviar.

4. The Danish author Theodore Reinking was forced to eat his own words. In 1644 he wrote a book entitled *Dania ad exteros de perfidia Suecorum*, which lamented the diminished fortunes of the Danes after their defeat by their neighbours, Sweden, in the 30 Years' War. It offended the Swedes so much that he was imprisoned for life. After several years in jail, he was given a straight choice: eat your book or lose your head. He chose the former.

5. In 1994 fisherman Renato Arganza spent several days at sea clinging to a buoy after his boat capsized off the Philippines. On being rescued he remarked that he had survived by eating his underpants.

6. Henry Ford I took to eating weed sandwiches every day when he heard that the American scientist George Washington Grover did the same.

7. During widespread food shortages in Cuba in 1994 the cat population fell by 400,000.

8. For the last 15 years of his life Howard Hughes lived almost exclusively on ice-cream. He generally stuck to the same flavor until every supplier in the district had run out.

9. Even at a time in Roman history known for culinary decadence, the Emperor Heliogabalus was renowned for his adventurous diet, dining on such delicacies as heads of parrot, flamingo brains, thrush brains and camel heels. At one feast he astonished his guests by serving up 600

flamingo heads, from which guests were expected to scoop out and eat the brains with gold spoons.

10. Ernest Hemingway wrote all his works on a diet of peanut butter sandwiches.

Death Row Cuisine: 10 Last Meals of Condemned Murderers

~

1. Ham, eggs, toast and coffee – Gee Jon, Chinese murderer, the first man ever to be executed in the US by lethal gas, at Carson City State Prison in 1924.

2. Hot fudge sundae – Barbara Graham, convicted murderess, executed by lethal gas at San Quintin, California, in 1955.

3. Steak and chips followed by peach cobbler dessert – murderer Charlie Brooks, executed by lethal injection at Huntsville, Texas, in 1982.

4. Cheez Doodles and Coca-Cola – mass poisoner Margaret Velma Barfield, a 52-year-old grandmother and the first woman ever to die by lethal injection, at Central Prison, North Carolina, in 1962.

5. Hamburger, eggs and potatoes – British killer Gary Gilmore, who became the first man to be executed in the US for a decade when he was shot dead by firing squad at Utah in 1977.

6. Candy – Chauncey Millard, the youngest person ever executed in the state of Utah, killed by firing squad in 1869. The 18-year-old was still eating his candy bar as he was being shot.

7. A large steak salad, potato pancakes and two helpings of jelly and ice-cream – Isadore Zimmerman, a 26-year-old convicted of murder, at Sing Sing in 1939. Zimmerman continued to protest his innocence to the last mouthful.

8. A US one dollar bill sandwich – Joshua Jones, hanged at Pennsylvania in 1839 for the murder of his wife. While Jones was awaiting execution he sold his body to the prison doctors for 10 dollars. He spent nine dollars on delicacies to vary his prison diet. Realizing that he still had a dollar bill in his pocket just minutes before his execution, he requested two slices of bread.

9. Two hamburgers and Coca-Cola – Leslie B. Gireth, executed at San Quintin in 1943 for the murder of his girlfriend. Gireth had lost his nerve halfway through a suicide pact with her. His last meal was an exact replica of what she had eaten just before he shot her.

10. Garlic bread, shrimp, French fries, ice-cream, strawberries and whipped cream – the heroic last order of Perry Smith and Richard Eugene Hickock, before their double hanging at Kansas in 1965. Sadly, they completely lost their appetites at the last minute and the meal was untouched.

Cereal Killers: 10 Victims of Food Rage

❧

1. Restaurant-owner Gilbert Menezes was sent for trial in 1996 for killing his wife's lover, then serving his liver, with fried onions, to his customers.

2. In 1984 Argentinian police found a set of bones belonging to a missing 19-year-old, Carlos Sanchez, beneath a Buenos Aires building which was used by devil worshippers. The occupants explained that they had phoned an order for pizzas, but after an interminable delay had decided to eat the delivery boy instead.

3. In Perth, Australia, in 1994 street trader Igor Roskny was beaten to death by an irate customer because he put mustard on his tuna sandwich by mistake. The murderer complained that he had clearly requested mayonnaise.

4. In January 1995 an Egyptian threw his wife from the window of their second-floor Cairo flat because his dinner wasn't ready. She suffered

concussion and multiple fractures: he was freed on £8 bail.

5. Thirty-one-year-old Brenda Hunter, of Zion, Illinois, shot her brother in 1994 because she disliked the type of cheese he was putting on their chilli dinner.

6. Heinrich Gembach of Munich choked his wife to death in 1995 by force-feeding her wheat cereal. He told police that this was what she had given him for breakfast every morning for the last 10 years.

7. In 1994 Peter Weiller, a German film-goer, was beaten to death by ushers in a Bonn cinema because he had brought his own popcorn.

8. The Sioux Chief "Rain In The Face" admitted that after the Battle of Little Big Horn in 1877 he had cut out General Custer's heart and eaten it. He said he didn't much like the taste of human flesh – he just wanted revenge.

9. A Frenchman, Noël Carriou, killed both of his wives because they were poor cooks. Fifty-four-year-old Carriou was sentenced to eight years in jail in 1978 after killing his second wife for cooking him an overdone roast. Seventeen years earlier he had broken his first wife's neck after she served him an undercooked meal. In passing sentence the judge sympathized with Carriou: good cooking, he agreed, was an important part of married life.

10. Ghengis Khan killed his own brother in an argument over a fish.

10 Gross World Eating Records

~

3.5 lb of cooked dog in 18 minutes, 10 seconds.

12 slugs in 2 minutes.

28 cockroaches in 4 minutes.

60 earthworms in 3 minutes, 6 seconds.

100 live maggots in 5 minutes, 29 seconds.

2 lb of eels in 32 seconds.

144 snails in 11 minutes, 30 seconds.

13 raw eggs in 1.4 seconds.

24 hot dogs in 12 minutes.

15 bowls of noodle soup, 100 pieces of sushi, 5 plates of wheat noodles, 5 plates of beef with rice, and 5 plates of curry and rice in 2 hours (Japanese national eating championships).

8 Last Suppers

~

1. Buddha died at the age of 80 in 483 BC, from an intestinal haemorrhage after eating a hot curry.

2. Elvis Presley: fried banana and peanut butter sandwich.

3. King John: dropped dead at an abbey in East Anglia, England, after gorging on peaches and cider.

4. Robert Maxwell: drowned on two bananas.

5. King George I: melon.

6. King Henry I: "a surfeit of lampreys."

7. British prime minister William Pitt the Younger: his last words were "I think I could eat one of Bellamy's veal pies."

8. Robert Greene, sixteenth-century English dramatist and pamphleteer: expired after consuming too much Rhenish wine and pickled herring at an author's gala luncheon.

10 All-Time most Disgusting Beverages

~

1. China produces a Three Penis Wine, made from
    one part seal penis, one part dog penis and four
    parts deer penis. It is allegedly an effective cure
    for anaemia, shingles and memory loss, and is
    described as "robust and nutritious."

2. In Ireland, sheep droppings boiled in milk was
    once highly valued as a cure for whooping
    cough.

3. The world's most exclusive coffee is made from a
    bean which has already passed through the colon
    of a cat. The droppings of the Palm Civet wild-
    cat, indigenous to the coffee plantations of
    Sumatra, are sold at market at £150,000 per
    tonne. In Japan the coffee sells at about £10 a
    cup.

4. The Yukon Territory in Canada is home of the
    Sour Toe Cocktail, which has just two
    ingredients: an amputated human toe and the
    spirit of your choice. The only rule which has to

be observed is: "You can drink it fast, you can drink it slow, but the lips have got to touch the toe." The original artefact was discovered in a disused log cabin by a Mountie in 1973. It was used in the drink more than 700 times before it was accidentally swallowed by a miner.

5. The Cocoma tribe of Peru drank the ground-up bones of deceased relatives in a fermented brew, believing that it was much better for the dead to be inside a warm friend than outside in the cold earth.

6. Professional chariot-racers in Ancient Rome were encouraged to promote muscle growth by drinking a solution of dried boar's dung.

7. In 1885 the US army captain and part-time naturalist John Bourke published a detailed description of the Urine Dance of the Zuni Indians of New Mexico. Bourke related that he had been privileged to witness this unique ritual, which involved a dozen Zuni Indians dancing around a fire while drinking several gallons of

fresh urine. When the Zuni invited their guests to participate in a similar ceremony, this time involving human excrement, Bourke made his excuses and left.

8. Elizabethan women drank the urine of puppy dogs to improve their complexions.

9. After the Great Fire of London in 1666 the remains of the deceased former dean of St Paul's, John Colet, were rescued from the cathedral where they had lain since 1509. Although they were protected by a lead-lined coffin, it was noted by two gentlemen named Wyld and Greatorex that the dean's remains had become cooked in his preserving fluids and had dissolved into a soupy substance like "boiled brawne." They tasted the "soup" and declared that it tasted "only of iron."

10. When Admiral Horatio Nelson died his corpse was placed in a keg of brandy to preserve it on the long journey home. Although the admiral's body had been bubbling away in it for days, this

didn't prevent his crew from drinking the spirits later.

10 Human Recipes

～

1. In 1996 the victim of a Japanese gangland killing, Shoichi Murakami, was hacked to pieces and his hands were used to make soup of the day in a local restaurant. The starter was eaten by about 50 satisfied customers.

2. Captain James Cook, the great explorer who had often written in his journals about the cannibalistic habits of some of the natives he encountered, almost certainly ended his days as an Hawaiian buffet. All that Cook's men could find of him after he had been killed and dismembered at a heianu ceremony at Keala Kekua were a few bones and some salted flesh.

3. The nineteenth-century English eccentric William Buckland claimed he ate the heart of King Louis XIV of France. The organ was allegedly plundered from the Sun King's grave during the French Revolution and had found its way onto Buckland's plate via his friend, the Archbishop of York.

4. During World War II the British Minister of Food, Lord Woolton, carefully considered but finally rejected a plan, proposed by his government scientists, to feed the country on black pudding made from surplus human blood bank donations.

5. According to West Indian cannibals, the tastiest bits on a human being are the palms of the hands, the fingers and toes.

6. One of Chicago's master butchers of the 1870s was the German Adolph Luetgert, whose driving ambition was to make his sausages famous all over America. Luetgert's dream came true. He was arrested and tried for the murder of his wife Louisa after disposing of her corpse by melting it down in one of his giant vats and incorporating her into his sausage production line. For two years after Leutgert's conviction, sausage sales in Illinois and neighboring Michigan hit an all-time low.

7. The Carib Indians of the West Indies, first discovered by Columbus, were the cannibal world connoisseurs of human *haute cuisine*: the local word for "Carib" is *Caniba* – the origin of the word cannibal. Caribs even bred children expressly for consumption: the children were first castrated because it improved the flavor. Columbus noted that the Caribs considered the French to be the very tastiest people in the world.

8. Marco Polo noted in 1275 that the people of southeast Asia ate the feet of their captives, believing them to be "the most savory food in the world."

9. The Tartar hordes who swept over Europe in 1242 were particularly fond of girls. Appetizing young maidens were issued as rations to army officers, while common soldiers chewed on the tough flesh of older women. Breast meat was regarded as the finest titbit, and was reserved for the prince's table.

10. Sir John Franklin, one of the greatest British Arctic explorers, was probably eaten by Eskimos or by his fellow adventurers. Sir John and his crew of 129 men perished attempting to walk across 1,000 miles of the Arctic Circle in 1847 after abandoning their ice-bound ship.

10 Bowel Problems

1. King Edmund Ironside: reign curtailed when an assassin thrust his longsword up the Saxon king's fundament.

2. King Edward II: assassinated by having a red-hot poker thrust up his rectum.

3. Samuel Pepys: "Wind doth now and then torment me about the fundament extremely."

4. King Louis XIV: flatulence. It was said that he conveyed his admiration for his sister-in-law the Duchess of Orleans by doing her the honor of farting loudly in her presence.

5. Martin Luther: suffered from chronic constipation.

6. King Ferdinand I of Naples: constipation. The daily bowel movements of the eighteenth-century monarch were an utterly serious business: he always insisted on having a crowd of

people around to keep him entertained while he strained. His father-in-law, the Austrian Emperor Joseph, was one of many who became privy to these unusual audiences, and noted later, "We made conversation for more than half an hour, and I believe he would still be there if a terrible stench had not convinced us that all was over." Ferdinand evidently also offered to show his father-in-law the fruit of his labors for closer inspection.

7. French Emperor Louis Napoleon III of France: suffered from a variety of ailments, including dysentery, gonorrhoea and a huge bladder stone. He commanded his troops at the Battle of Sedan in 1870 with towels stuffed inside his breeches to act as king-size nappies.

8. Queen Victoria: she ate too quickly, mixed malt whisky with claret, and was a martyr to persistent flatulence.

9. Adolf Hitler: flatulence. His personal doctor Theodore Morrell gave him "anti-gas" medication to allay the Führer's embarrassment.

10. Elvis Presley: became addicted to Freenamint chewing gum whilst attempting to overcome his severe constipation.

Chapter 2

LOVE HURTS

Adorable Ewe: 10 Animal Passions

～

1. One of the least publicized examples of Ice Age cave art depicts a man on skis having sex with an elk. Middle Eastern cave paintings also reveal that men once believed that sex with female crocodiles would bring them success in life.

2. The Incas had laws to prevent llama drivers from having sex with their animals: they enforced them by requiring that llama drivers were escorted by chaperones.

3. Frederick the Great, who never slept with his wife, was rumored in later years to have been romantically attached to his pack of Italian whippet bitches.

4. In 1857 Warren Drake, a soldier serving in the Utah militia in Echo Canyon, was found guilty of having sexual relations with a mare. A court martial sentenced both Drake and the mare to death. The soldier's sentence was subsequently commuted to exile from the territory; the less fortunate mare was executed.

5. In 1952 a man from Nigeria was accused of committing an act of sexual indecency with a pigeon in Hyde Park. His resourceful defence counsel reminded the judge of a precedent in the 1930s, when a man was accused of buggering a duck: on that occasion the accused had escaped scot-free after pointing out that a duck was a fowl, not a beast, and that he was therefore innocent of the charge of bestiality. The case against the Nigerian was dismissed, although he was fined £10 for taking the pigeon home and eating it.

6. In December 1993 James Humfleet, 33, was charged with the murder of his uncle, Samuel Humfleet. According to the accused he became angry after stumbling across his uncle having sex with one of the two pit bulls belonging to the owner of the trailer in which they had been partying.

7. In Key West, Florida, Patricia Wyatt called local police to report a stray pot-bellied pig having sex with her husband's new Harley Davidson. While trying to mate with the motorcycle's front wheel,

the 50-pound pig scratched the paintwork, causing at least $100 damage. Animal control officers were uncertain as to what action to take against the pig. The bike's owner, Walter Wyatt, complained: "His crime is an alleged sex act against a Harley. We don't even know if that's a felony."

8. A man from Silver Spring, Maryland, became infected with rabies in 1996 after he admitted having sex with a deceased racoon. He was charged with animal cruelty.

9. In Lebanon a man may legally have sex with an animal so long as it is female.

10. In August 1996 a court in Eagleville, Tennessee, charged a man with indecent exposure when it was discovered that the state had no law to apply to the act of having sexual intercourse with a miniature horse.

9 Historical Figures who Died during Sexual Intercourse

1. Attila the Hun. Although short, squat and extremely ugly, Attila had a dozen wives. He burst an artery on his wedding night with his 12th.

2. Pope Leo VII (936–9) died of a heart attack during sex.

3. Pope John VII (955–64) was bludgeoned to death by the cuckolded husband of the woman he was making love with at the time.

4. Pope John XIII (965–72) was also murdered by an irate husband who discovered His Holiness on top of his wife.

5. Pope Paul II (1467–71) allegedly died of a heart attack while being sodomized by a page boy.

6. The Duke of Orleans, Regent to the French boy-king Louis XV. In 1721 the depraved and elderly duke took a new mistress who was nearly 30 years younger than him, against the advice of his doctors. He was found slumped by the fireplace of his drawing-room one day dying from a massive stroke.

7. French president Félix Faure (1841–99) died during sex in a Paris brothel. Faure's death sent the woman into shock and his member had to be surgically removed from her.

8. Lord Palmerston, British prime minister (1855–8, 1859–65) died of a heart attack while having sex with a young parlor maid on his billiard table on 18 October 1865.

9. Nelson Rockefeller, a former US vice-president, died aged 71 while copulating with his mistress.

10 Aphrodisiacs

1. At one time Chinese emperors were required to keep 121 wives – a precise number thought to have magical properties – 10 of whom the emperor was expected to make love to every night. A Taoist manual advised that this could be made possible by applying sheep's eyelid marinaded in hot tea to the imperial penis.

2. Menstrual blood as a food or drink additive (Germany, eighteenth century).

3. Live monkey brains (Malaysia). The monkey was forced into a tight container to prevent it from escaping, and a bowl fitted to its head. The live monkey suffered agony while its scalp was cut open and peeled back to reveal the exposed brain. The brain was then scooped out with a spoon or sucked through a straw.

4. Toad excrement (France, eighteenth century). This method was also once used by Louis XIV's

ageing mistress Madame de Montespan to revive the Sun King's flagging interest in her.

5. Lion testicles or arsenic (Regency London).

6. Penis and scrotum of a vanquished enemy warrior (Brazilian Cubeo tribe, nineteenth century).

7. Dolphin's testicles (Japan). Chicken testicles are preferred in Taiwan.

8. Pigeon dung and snail excrement (medieval England).

9. Animal hormone. To maintain Adolf Hitler's impaired virility, his personal physician Dr Theodore Morrell injected the Führer with a compound containing hormones from crushed animal genitalia.

10. Chilli and hot spices: banned from Peruvian prison food because they are likely to arouse passions "unseemly in a single-sex environment."

Safe Sex: History's 10 Most Original Contraceptive Devices

~

1. Pessaries made from crocodile dung (ancient Egypt) or from goats' bladders (ancient Rome).

2. Sixteen tadpoles fried in quicksilver, to be swallowed quickly by the woman immediately after intercourse (ancient China).

3. Spitting three times in the mouth of a frog, or eating bees immediately after intercourse (Dominican Church, thirteenth century).

4. Mashed pomegranate mixed with rock salt and alum (ancient Arabia).

5. Drinking raw onion juice (Europe, sixteenth century).

6. Ingesting cabbage immediately after intercourse (Europe, seventeenth century).

7. Jumping backwards seven or nine times immediately after sexual intercourse (Islamic, eighteenth century).

8. Condoms made from animal offal (Europe, eighteenth century). The original condoms were made by slaughterhouse workers from sausage skins. The modern variety did not become popular until Mr Goodyear vulcanized rubber in 1843. In Japan, men continued to wear sheaths made from leather or tortoiseshell.

9. Because he hated using condoms, Casanova placed his faith in a technique by which he inserted into his partner three gold balls, purchased from a Genoese goldsmith for about £50. He claimed that this method had served him well for 15 years. A more likely explanation for his run of luck is that he was infertile.

10. In some Third World countries the use of cola as a douche is one of the most common and successful forms of contraceptive. Scientifically controlled tests at Harvard Medical School proved that although regular cola has a 91 per cent success rate as spermicide, the diet variety is 100 per cent effective.

10 All-Time Least Romantic Honeymoons

~

1. George Albert Crossman and his wife Ellen Sampson, a nurse, were married in January 1903. The morning after their wedding night they had an argument which resulted in Crossman killing his bride by smashing her skull in with a hammer. He hid the body in a tin box in an upstairs room at their home in Kensal Rise, London, where it remained for the next 15 months. For most of this time he was living with another woman, Edith Thompson. Eventually, a lodger named William Dell complained about the smell seeping into his digs. When the police closed in, Crossman slit his own throat with a razor.

2. In August 1994 Minnesota newly-wed Gregory McCloud broke his back while carrying his 20-stone bride Helen over the threshold. Doctors described the 10-stone groom's injuries as being consistent with those of someone who had been crushed by a car.

3. Cesare Borgia, the son of the early sixteenth-century Pope Alexander V, had his wedding night wrecked when a practical joker switched his regular medication for a bottle of laxative pills.

4. German-born Amy Weltz went to her wedding in Brisbane in September 1993 unaware of the Australian tradition of smearing wedding cake in your spouse's face. When her new husband Chas rubbed a slice of wedding cake in her face during the reception she quickly responded by smashing a bottle over his head, killing him almost instantly.

5. On his wedding night the Victorian author and critic John Ruskin found the sight of his wife's pubic hair so shocking that he vowed never to sleep with her again.

6. King George IV nearly fainted when he first clapped eyes on his obese, ugly and sweaty wife Caroline of Brunswick-Wolfenbüttel the day before they were due to be married. On their wedding night he got himself blind drunk so that

he could tolerate her "personal nastiness" long enough to sleep with her once — after which the couple went their separate ways, never once attempting to disguise their mutual loathing. When Napoleon Bonaparte died in 1821, a messenger rushed to inform the king: "Your Majesty, your greatest enemy is dead." George replied, "Is she, by God?"

7. A young Japanese couple, Sachi and Tomio Hidaki, were married in 1978, but they were so shy that they didn't get around to consummating their marriage for another 14 years. Sadly, the excitement of enjoying normal marital relations for the first time was too much for them and they both died of heart attacks.

8. On 11 June 1983, Moses Alexander, aged 93, was married to Frances Tompkins, aged 105, in New York. The next morning the newly-weds were removed, both of them dead, from their marital bed.

9. John Harvey Kellogg was the inventor of the cereal flake. On his wedding night with Ella

Eaton he spent all evening writing *Plain Facts for Old and Young*, a 644-page treatise on the evils of sexual intercourse. This included a 97-page essay, "Secret Vice (Solitary Vice or Self-Abuse): its Symptoms and Results." Kellogg listed 39 tell-tale signs indicating that someone was masturbating, including sleeplessness, love of solitude, unnatural boldness, confusion of ideas, use of tobacco and acne. The marriage was never consummated.

10. According to royal biographer Andrew Morton, as a special honeymoon treat, Prince Charles allowed Diana to lie in the Balmoral heather while he read her passages from the works of Carl Jung and Laurens van der Post.

History's 50 most Famous Syphilitics

1. Pope Alexander VI.

2. Ludwig van Beethoven.

3. Emil von Behring.

4. Queen Cleopatra.

5. Christopher Columbus.

6. Al Capone.

7. King Charles VIII of France.

8. King Christian VII of Denmark.

9. Randolph Churchill.

10. Emperor Commodus.

11. Captain James Cook.

12. Frederick Delius.

13. Albrecht Dürer.

14. Queen Elizabeth I.

15. Desiderius Erasmus.

16. King François I of France.

17. King Frederick II the Great of Prussia.

18. King Frederick V of Denmark.

19. Paul Gauguin.

20. King George I.

21. Johann Wolfgang von Goethe.

22. Francisco Goya.

23. Heinrich Heine.

24. King Henry VIII.

25. King Herod of Judaea.

26. Adolf Hitler.

27. Czar Ivan the Terrible.

28. King James II.

29. Pope Julius II.

30. Julius Caesar.

31. John Keats.

32. Pope Leo X.

33. Ferdinand Magellan.

34. Emperor Marcus Aurelius.

35. Mary Queen of Scots.

36. Guy de Maupassant.

37. John Milton.

38. Edouard Monet.

39. Benito Mussolini.

40. Friedrich Nietzsche.

41. Czar Paul I.

42. Czar Peter the Great.

43. Cardinal Richelieu.

44. Marquis de Sade.

45. Franz Schubert.

46. Arthur Schopenhauer.

47. Jonathan Swift.

48. Emperor Tiberius.

49. Henri Toulouse-Lautrec.

50. Oscar Wilde.

10 Crimes of Passion

1. Patricia Orionno was France's least competent murderess. In 1988 she decided to get rid of her husband because he made excessive sexual demands of her. She tried to kill him with sleeping tablets, but underestimated the dosage and only made him oversleep. She slashed his wrists, tried to gas him, then tried to smother him with a pillow. She was successful in her fifth attempt, stabbing him eight times. She was subsequently freed when the French judge ruled that it was a crime of passion.

2. When King John of England found out that his wife Isabella had taken a lover, he had him killed and his corpse strung up over Isabella's side of the bed.

3. Regina Chatien, 43, and Melvin Hoffman, 53, were each fined $1,000 for engaging in oral sex during a 1995 football game at the Los Angeles Dodger Stadium, while in attendance with their four children.

4. In July 1996 Gail Murphy, 47, of Brooklyn, New York, was arrested for shooting her husband dead because he had gone on a six-hour fishing trip while she was recovering from haemorrhoid surgery. A police investigator explained to the *New York Times*: "She felt that her husband didn't demonstrate that he cared for her on that particular day."

5. Jeffrey Watkins, 24, was convicted in 1994 of breaking into five New York mausoleums and stealing the skull of a woman who had been dead since 1933. Watkins confessed that he had slept with remains inside coffins: "I feel safe with the dead, and I can trust them. I need their company to make me peaceful inside."

6. To see if he could get a reaction from his unfaithful wife, the Russian czar Peter the Great had the head of her suspected lover pickled in alcohol and placed in a jar at her bedside.

7. In 1994, when the wife of Polish adulterer Boris Paveharik found a pack of condoms in her husband's pocket, she filled them with ground

pepper. After the next visit to his mistress Mr Paveharik was rushed to hospital suffering severe swelling and inflammation.

8. A 67-year-old American, Marland Maynard, was convicted of the manslaughter of his wife Maybel in 1995. The court heard that Maynard had returned home from work to find his wife in the act of attempting suicide with a handgun. When the gun jammed, Marland helped her reload it.

9. Three months after the burial of his fiancée, Roberto Carlos da Silva, 21, of Socorcaba, Brazil, dug up her body, which was wearing a wedding dress, and had sex with it. He told the Estado news agency: "I was desperate and needed her."

10. Thai Buddhist monk Sayan Duriyalak was so outraged by the discovery that his 67-year-old abbot was violating his vow of chastity by having an affair with a 51-year-old nun that he attacked the couple with an axe while they made love, decapitating the abbot and seriously

wounding the nun. Sayan told police that he had planned his attack to imitate an execution he had recently seen on a TV cop series.

Get your Teeth out for the Lads:
10 Libidinous Geriatrics

～

1. In September 1996 a male inmate died of a cardiac arrest and five more were treated for palpitations after a 79-year-old woman stripped off in a home for the elderly in Brisbane, Australia.

2. In 1993 a police raid on the A-1 Massage Studio in Oregon, US, uncovered a masturbation service offered by two sisters, aged 70 and 73.

3. In 1994 Los Angeles police were alerted to find a peeping Tom. Apparently the man specialized in dressing up as the grim reaper, with a scythe in his hand, and staring through the windows of nursing homes at old inmates.

4. In 1981 French magistrates gave an 80-year-old prostitute a 10-month suspended prison sentence. The Paris court heard that Madame

Marie Louise Soccodato had been plying her trade since 1941, although lately business had been dropping off.

5. A 72-year-old doctor caused a sensation in 1889 when he gave a lecture to the French Society of Biology about his discovery of the elixir of youth. Dr Charles Brown-Séquard described how he chopped and ground up the testicles of puppies and guinea pigs, then injected himself with the resulting compound. He announced that he was now physically 30 years younger and boasted that he was able to "visit" his young wife every day without fail. The lecture caused a stir in the medical establishment, albeit briefly: soon afterwards his wife left him for a younger man, and shortly after that the doctor dropped dead from a cerebral haemorrhage.

6. Catherine the Great of Russia was both an insomniac and a nymphomaniac, which was very bad news for the dozens of handsome young soldiers she continued to bed well into her 70s. She advocated sexual intercourse six times a day,

had 21 "official" lovers and employed a doctor to examine all new applicants.

7. The Russian surgeon Serge Voronoff started to study Egyptian court eunuchs when it occurred to him that most of them looked remarkably good for their age, and concluded that male sex glands rejuvenated the body. In 1920 he put his theories to the test: he took the testicles of a chimpanzee and grafted them onto a 73-year-old man. Voronoff recorded that his experiment only had "a temporary effect."

8. In accordance with the fashion of the day, unmarried Elizabethan women wore their breasts exposed – a habit Queen Elizabeth herself favored well into her 70s.

9. Chairman Mao regularly suffered from venereal disease, but refused to be treated or to abstain from sex until the infection cleared. The young girls whom he continued to bed well into his 70s considered catching VD from their chairman a badge of honour and testimony to their close personal relationships with Mao.

10. In Iran in 1994 Mohammad Esmail al-Bahrami, aged 105, filed for divorce from his wife, Fatemeh Razavi, aged 100.

Chapter 3

COURTING THE MUSE

10 Hard Acts to Follow:

~

1. A Beatles tribute band lost its "George Harrison" in a tragic motorway accident in 1994. The "quiet Beatle," a.k.a. 27-year-old Duncan Bloomfield, fell out of the back of their transit van on the M40 while the band was travelling home from a performance in London. The rest of the band had driven for 25 miles before they realized that he was missing.

2. Richard Versalle, a tenor performing at the New York Metropolitan Opera House in 1995, suffered a heart attack and fell 10 feet from a ladder to the stage after singing the line "You can only live so long" from the opening scene of *The Makropulos Case*, a Czech opera about an elixir that confers eternal youth.

3. The US actor Lorne Greene had one of his nipples bitten off by an alligator while filming *Lorne Greene's Wild Kingdom*.

4. The American stage actress Annie von Behein was performing in the Coliseum Theater, Cincinatti, in a drama called *Si Slocum*, in which her real-life fiancé, Frank Frayne, was required to shoot an apple from her head, *à la* William Tell, with a musket. Frayne shot too low and the 2,300-strong audience watched as the musket ball hit her neatly in the forehead. She died 15 minutes later, while the audience was still leaving the theater.

5. In October 1980 an Indian mystic, Khadeshwari Baba, attempted to show off his incredible powers of meditation by remaining buried alive in a 10-foot-deep pit for 10 days. In a carnival-like atmosphere a crowd of over 1,000 people, including several local officials from the town of Gorakhpur, watched as Baba was ceremoniously lowered into the pit, and the hole was filled in behind him. Ten days later the pit was re-opened. From the accompanying stench it was estimated that the mystic had been dead for at least a week.

6. American Orville Stamm entertained by lying on his back with a piano on his chest. While Orville sang, the pianist would bounce up and down on his thighs, belting out the tune to "Ireland Must Be Heaven Because Mother Comes From There."

7. One of the world's most tasteless stage acts was performed by the American Tommy Minnock, a variety artiste who plied his trade in Trenton, New Jersey, in the 1890s. Minnock allowed himself to be literally crucified onstage: while the nails were being driven into his hands and feet, he would entertain his audience by signing *After The Ball Is Over*.

8. The 1954 film epic about Genghis Khan, *The Conqueror* starring John Wayne, was made near a nuclear testing site in Utah's Escalante Desert within months of an atomic explosion. Over the next few decades cancer claimed the lives of several members of the cast and crew, including Wayne, the director/producer Dick Powell, co-stars Susan Hayward and Agnes Moorehead,

and Pedro Armendariz, who shot himself when he learned he had the disease.

9. In 1994 health department workers fumigated the San Francisco Opera House after musicians complained of itching, caused by scabies. It was reported that some violinists had to drop their bows during performances in order to scratch.

10. The original cast of the US sitcom *Friends* had a seventh regular member, Marcel the monkey. He was fired because of his habit of vomiting live worms on the set.

In the Best Possible Bad Taste:
10 Conceptual Artists

~

1. Piero Manzoni, sixties artist, and the sole exponent of the art movement *arte povera*, exhibited cans of his own excrement.

2. Louise Bourgeois, a Canadian feminist sculptor, creates work featuring severed penises and huge testicles hanging singly or in pairs or bunches, including a piece called *No Exit* – a stairway with two huge testicles restricting egress at the bottom – and *Untitled (with Foot)*, in which a baby is crushed by a large testicle.

3. Richard Gibson, another Canadian sculptor, exhibits pieces made from freeze-dried human body parts, especially limbs and ears. In 1986 he advertized for spare parts and was arrested and fined £500 for conduct likely to cause a breach of the peace.

4. In 1994 Ronnie Nicolino, the Californian artist, created a two-mile-long sand sculpture comprising 21,000 size 34C breasts. Nicolino said that his next project would be a giant chain of bras long enough to span the Grand Canyon, adding that in no way was he obsessed with breasts.

5. Gilbert and George, British artists, once staged a show at the South London Art Gallery which they called *Naked Shit Pictures*, comprising 16 large glossy photos of themselves surrounded by a series of "defecation motifs," including turd circles and turd sculptures. One critic described the work as "almost biblical."

6. Catherine Gregory's 1992 exhibition in Scarborough featured a dismembered dog chopped into nine pieces and suspended from the ceiling, 63 squashed mice mounted in plastic and the butchered remains of three rabbits. She said she did it for the animal rights movement.

7. In 1996 Brigid Berlin, the New York artist, showcased her collection of 500 photographs of penises, contributed by people she had met in the early 1970s during her acquaintance with Andy Warhol. She was previously known for her Tit Prints drawings, using her nipples instead of brushes, and her Penis Pillows – photomontages of penises, photocopied and stuffed into plastic pillows.

8. Newton Harrison, an American artist, staged an art exhibition called *Portable Fish Farm* in 1971 at the Hayward Gallery, London, at which he planned to publicly electrocute 60 live catfish. The electrocution was finally called off after a protest by Spike Milligan, who made his feelings known by lobbing a brick through the Hayward Gallery window.

9. Hermann Nitsch, an Austrian artist, staged a performance in 1975 using a dead bull and 11 deceased sheep.

10. In 1994 Christian Lemmerz, a Danish artist, put six dead pigs in a glass case so that visitors to the Ezbjerg gallery could watch them change color from a piggy-pink to black, via various shades of blue and grey. The artist declared it a triumph for people who value reality in art. The gallery owners said it was a triumph over their old ventilation system, which was unable to cope with the stench.

10 Classical Composers
who didn't make it to their 40th Birthday
~

1. Vincenzo Bellini (died at 33).

2. Georges Bizet (36).

3. Frédéric Chopin (39).

4. George Gershwin (38).

5. Felix Mendelssohn (38).

6. Wolfgang Amadeus Mozart (35).

7. Giovanni Battista Pergolesi (26).

8. Henry Purcell (36).

9. Franz Schubert (31).

10. Carl Maria von Weber (39).

10 Musical Bans

1. In the fourth century BC Plato called for a ban on certain types of contemporary music from the Greek republic because he believed that pop music led to low morals.

2. In 1936 Adolf Hitler banned music by Mendelssohn because the composer was Jewish.

3. In 1963 *Dominique*, by The Singing Nun, was banned by Springfield, Massachusetts, station WHYN, because it was "degrading to Catholics."

4. In 1969 *Je T'Aime ... Moi Non Plus* by Jane Birkin and Serge Gainsbourg was banned by US and European radio stations for content of an explicit sexual nature.

5. In 1962 *Speedy Gonzales*, an innocuous novelty single by the bland US crooner Pat Boone, was considered offensive to Mexicans and banned in the US.

6. In 1966 The Beatles accidentally snubbed Imelda Marcos at Manila airport and were banned in the Philippines.

7. In 1966 The Beatles' *A Day In The Life* was widely banned because of alleged drug references.

8. In 1968 Communist party leader Chairman Mao Tse-Tung banned *The Sound of Music* in China because it was a blatant example of capitalist pornography.

9. In 1984 the year's best-selling UK record, *Relax*, by Frankie Goes to Hollywood, was played by BBC Radio 1 for several weeks before D.J. Mike Read discovered that the lyrics were about gay sex.

10. In 1994 Dudley and District Hospital Radio banned the Frank Sinatra standard *My Way* from their airwaves because the lines "And now the end is near/And so I face the final curtain" were considered too depressing for terminally ill patients. Other suggested NHS record bans

include Tony Bennett's *I Left My Heart In San Francisco* – too distressing for coronary patients – and Andy Fairweather-Low's *Wide Eyed and Legless* – unsuitable for amputees.

1. In 1863 the authoress Louisa May Alcott fell ill, and noted in her journal that she suffered from terrible hallucinations, in which she was repeatedly molested by a big Spaniard with soft hands. She recovered and went on to write *Little Women*.

2. The mad nineteenth-century French poet Gérard de Nerval could occasionally be seen taking a lobster for a walk on the end of a length of ribbon. After being institutionalized eight times he was discovered dead, hanging from a Paris lamp post in 1855.

3. The schizophrenic German composer Robert Schumann had two imaginary friends called Florestan and Eusebius, who gave him ideas for his scores. Schumann died in an insane asylum.

4. The nineteenth-century French writer Honoré de Balzac believed that sex was a drain on his creativity. After several months of abstinence he

was once tempted into a Paris brothel, but moaned later: "I lost a novel this morning."

5. Samuel Johnson wrote *Rasselas* in seven days flat to pay for his mother's funeral.

6. Arnold Bennett's novels were renowned for attention to detail. Once he was complimented on his description of the death of Darius Clayhanger in the Clayhanger series, a death scene acclaimed as the most realistic of its kind in the history of English literature. Bennett explained later how this had been possible: "All the time my father was dying I was at the bedside making copious notes."

7. The eighteenth-century artist Benjamin West had an executed criminal exhumed and crucified to see how he hung.

8. Gustav Mahler, famous for his funeral marches, suffered from depression and had a morbid fixation about death. He wrote his first funeral march when he was six.

9. Algernon Charles Swinburne's Victorian public schooling left him with an addiction to flagellation. He was an avid reader of the Marquis de Sade and regularly visited a London flogging house. His tribute to the joy of whipping, *The Flogging Block*, now resides in the British Museum.

10. From childhood the Victorian nonsense poet and artist Edward Lear suffered from what he called "the Demon" – epilepsy – and "the Morbids" – manic depression – both of which he always maintained were the result of excessive masturbation.

10 Essential Elvis Facts

~

1. Before discovering Elvis, Colonel Tom Parker's most notable success was "Colonel Parker's Dancing Chickens," an act which involved persuading chickens to perform by sticking them on an electric hotplate.

2. There are an estimated 48,000 Elvis impersonators worldwide. In the Islamic state of Mogadishu in Somalia, it is illegal to impersonate Elvis without a beard.

3. The ghost of Elvis has possessed the TV remote control in a woman's house in Memphis, Tennessee. According to Phyllis Callas, whenever she watches television the channel starts changing to football games by itself, toilets rattle and doors slam. There is also a stain on the patio door in the image of the King. The house was originally owned by Elvis at the beginning of the 1960s, and backs onto his Graceland estate. A local School for Psychics performed an energy scan over the property and

confirmed that Elvis's spirit does visit occasionally.

4. Death was Elvis's best ever career move: had he lived he would almost certainly have been bankrupt within six months.

5. Elvis would also have had a problem with political correctness: just about the only thing that would prevent him from seducing a woman was knowing that she had been with a black man.

6. The First Presleyterian Church of Elvis the Divine was formed in the US in 1988. Among the King's 31 Commandments: Eat six meals a day.

7. The King's favorite snacks included fried peanut butter and banana sandwiches, burnt bacon, lemon meringue pie, and cornbread in buttermilk. He also had a fridge in his bedroom stocked with his favorite confectionery, Eskimo Pies and Nutty Buddys. In the 1970s his kitchen was manned 24 hours a day. The busiest time was around 4.30 am, when he liked to

binge on three double-decker cheeseburgers and six or seven banana splits. As Elvis was usually heavily sedated with his regular nightly cocktail of barbiturates and tranquillizers, his aides frequently had to save him from choking to death by reaching down his throat to remove food lodged in his windpipe.

8. During the last two and a half years of the King's life, his personal physician George Nichopoulos gave him about 20,000 doses of narcotics, stimulants, sedatives and anti-depressants, but Elvis had many other sources for his drugs, too. The pathologist who compiled the toxicology report after his death in 1977 testified that he had never before seen so many drugs in one body.

9. Next to sex and gluttony, his favorite nocturnal pastime was visiting the Memphis morgue to look at the corpses.

10. In July 1993 retired Texan US Air Force Major Bill Smith filed a lawsuit in Fort Worth against the estate of Elvis Presley. Major Smith charged

that Presley's estate had perpetrated a fraud by keeping up the pretence that the King had died in 1977. The major complained that this had interfered with his attempts to sell his new book on Elvis's current whereabouts.

10 Esoteric Works in the British Library

~

1. *The Romance of Leprosy*, E. Mackerchar, 1949.

2. *Why Bring That Up? A Guide to Seasickness*, J.F. Montague, 1936.

3. *Penetrating Wagner's Ring*, John L. Di Gaetanao, 1978.

4. *Constipation and Our Civilization*, J.C. Thomson, 1943.

5. *A Pictorial Book of Tongue Coating*, Anon., 1981.

6. *A Government Committee of Enquiry on the Light Metal Artificial Leg*, Captain Henry Hulme and Chisholm Baird, 1923.

7. *Daddy Was An Undertaker*, McDill, McGown and Gassman, 1952.

8. *Amputation Stumps: Their Care and After-treatment*, Sir Godfrey Martin Huggins, 1918.

9. *A Study of Masturbation and its Reputed Sequelae*, J.F.W. Meagher, 1924.

10. *Sex After Death*, B.J. Ferrell and D.E. Frey, 1983.

Dipped In Vitriol:
10 Writers On Writers

~

1. Jane Austen: "To me, Poe's prose is unreadable – like Jane Austen's. No, there is a difference. I could read his prose on a salary, but not Jane's." – *Mark Twain*

2. Ben Jonson: "Reading him is like wading through glue." – *Alfred, Lord Tennyson*

3. Alexander Pope: "There are two ways of disliking poetry. One way is to dislike it, the other is to read Pope." – *Oscar Wilde*

4. Robert Browning: "I don't think Browning was very good in bed. His wife probably didn't care for him very much. He snored and had fantasies about 12-year-old girls." – *W.H. Auden*

5. James Joyce: "The work of a queasy undergraduate scratching his pimples." – *Virginia Woolfe* on *Ulysses*

6. Arnold Bennett: "The Hitler of the book racket." – *Percy Wyndham Lewis*

7. Thomas Gray: "He was dull in company, dull in his closet, dull everywhere ... he was a mechanical poet." – *Samuel Johnson*

8. Ernest Hemingway: "When his cock wouldn't stand up he blew his head off. He sold himself a line of bullshit and he bought it." – *Germaine Greer*

9. Percy Bysshe Shelley: "A poor creature who has said or done nothing worth a serious man taking the trouble of remembering." – *Thomas Carlyle*

10. Dylan Thomas: "An outstandingly unpleasant man, one who cheated and stole from his friends and peed on their carpets." – *Kingsley Amis*

10 People Who Hated Shakespeare

1. Edward Young, British poet: "Shakespeare — what trash are his works in the gross."

2. Voltaire: "This enormous dunghill."

3. Leo Tolstoy: "Crude, immoral, vulgar and senseless."

4. George Bernard Shaw: "With the single exception of Homer, there is no eminent writer, not even Sir Walter Scott, whom I despise so entirely as I despise Shakespeare when I measure my mind against his. It would be positively a relief to me to dig him up and throw stones at him."

5. Walter Savage Landor, British poet: "The sonnets are hot and pothery, there is much condensation, little delicacy, like raspberry jam without cream, without crust, without bread."

6. Dr Samuel Johnson: "Shakespeare never had six lines together without a fault. Perhaps you may find seven, but this does not refute my general assertion."

7. Robert Greene, English playwright: "An upstart now beautified with our feathers."

8. Elizabeth Forsyth, English writer: "A sycophant, a flatterer, a breaker of marriage vows, a whining and inconsistent person."

9. Charles Darwin: "I have tried lately to read Shakespeare and found it so intolerably dull that it nauseated me."

10. King George III: "Is this not sad stuff, what what?"

Chapter 4

R.I.P.

Falling Between Stools:
10 Lavatorial Deaths

~

1. Roman emperor Heliogabalus (AD 204–222) was hacked to death by the praetorian guard as he sat on the lavatory, and his body thrown down a Roman sewer.

2. The Saxon king Edmund Ironside had his reign curtailed when he sat on a wooden lavatory: an assassin hiding in the pit below twice thrust his longsword up the king's anal passage, embedding the sword in his bowels and killing him instantly.

3. Russia's empress Catherine the Great died of heart failure while straining to overcome constipation.

4. King George II, according to his German *valet de chambre*, was a loud and garrulous farter. One evening he heard a roar from the palace privy which he judged to be "louder than the usual royal wind" and found the king slumped dead on

the floor. George had fallen off the toilet, smashing his head on a cabinet as he fell.

5. Sussex's messiest death occurred in 1856 when Matthew Gladman fell into a Lewes High Street cesspit. He had apparently entered a water closet in the dark, unaware that the floorboards had been removed in order to empty the chamber below. Doctors tried to revive him with electric shock therapy but failed. He died of asphyxiation by methane gas.

6. The 36-year-old Hollywood screen actress Lupe Velez, the "Mexican Spitfire," attempted to commit suicide by overdosing on sleeping pills in 1934. Ms Velez underestimated the dosage, however, and suddenly felt violently sick. As she made a dash for the bathroom she slipped on the tiled floor and was flung head first into her toilet. Her maid found her the next day with her head jammed down the bowl, drowned.

7. In 1957 King Haakon VII of Norway slipped on some soap in his marble bathroom and

smashed his head on some taps, fatally fracturing his skull.

8. Elvis Presley died of heart failure in 1977 and was found face down in his bathroom.

9. In September 1990 a joint reception in honour of the double wedding of two Jordanian brothers and their brides ended when the dance floor gave way, catapulting the entire wedding party into a cesspool below. Thirteen people died, including both brides.

10. A 41-year-old German, Heinz Schmitzer, fell into an outhouse cesspit in 1994 and drowned in raw sewage while attempting to retrieve his wallet.

10 Deaths Without Dignity

1. In July 1994, a 39-year-old motorcyclist in Commerce City, Colorado, was killed when a 40-pound dog fell off an overhead bridge on to his head, causing him to lose control of the bike and collide with a truck.

2. Pickles the dog, who discovered the Jules Rimet Trophy under a bush after it was stolen before the World Cup finals in 1966, strangled himself on his own lead while chasing a cat.

3. Sir Arthur Aston, Royalist commander during the English Civil War, was beaten to death with his own wooden leg by Cromwell's men.

4. The French composer Jean-Baptiste Lully accidentally stabbed himself in the foot with his baton and died of gangrene.

5. Sandra Orellana from Texas fell to her death from the eighth-floor balcony at the Industry Hills Sheraton, where she staying during a business conference in 1996. Police said Orellana fell accidentally as she and her boss Robert Salazar were having sex against a handrail, and she changed positions.

6. In October 1973, in accordance with his last wish, a Swedish confectionery salesman from Falkenberg, Roland Ohisson, was buried in a coffin made entirely of chocolate.

7. The jazz musician Joe "Poolie" Newman, trumpet-player with the likes of Count Basie and Lionel Hampton, was a notorious womanizer. In 1989 Newman, determined to live up to his reputation, tried to his enhance his flagging sex life with a penile implant. Unfortunately, a build-up of pressure caused his member to explode one evening while he was in a restaurant, and he haemorrhaged to death.

8. An Icelandic funeral parlor was fined in 1993 after the bereaved family of Henri Labonte complained to local authorities that the deceased had been dressed for his 26 December funeral in a Santa Claus costume and was wearing a fake beard.

9. Elizabeth, the wife of the poet and painter Dante Gabriel Rossetti, died in 1862 after overdosing on the laudanum she was taking for her neuralgia. Rossetti, himself an alcoholic and a morphine addict, was grief-stricken, and as a token of his love had a pile of his unpublished manuscripts wrapped in her golden tresses and buried with her in her coffin. Seven years later, however, he had a change of heart and decided that he wanted them back. Up came Elizabeth, and the poems were dusted off and published to great critical acclaim.

10. When King Francis I of Naples died, his corpse was embalmed and lay in state on display for three days, in accordance with royal custom. On

the third night the two sentries on duty beside him were startled by a thud: after closer inspection of the cask they deserted their post and ran screaming into the night. Apparently one of the king's arms had dropped off.

10 Celebrity Body Parts

1. Albert Einstein's eyes. Removed by his ophthalmologist Dr Henry Abrams during the autopsy in 1955 and stored in a safety deposit box. The eyes were put up for auction in 1994.

2. Napoleon Bonaparte's penis. Removed at autopsy by a team of French and Belgian doctors. When first put up for auction in 1972 at Christie's, the member was observed to be approximately one inch long and was listed as "a small, dried-up object." It failed to measure up to the reserve price and was withdrawn, but was bought five years later by an American urologist for $3,800.

3. Hitler's teeth. Used to positively identify his charred remains, which were discovered by Soviet soldiers in a shallow grave outside his Berlin bunker in 1945. They have remained locked away in an archive somewhere in Moscow ever since.

4. Elvis Presley's wart. Perhaps the most unique item of Elvis memorabilia, currently owned by Joni Mabe of Athens, Georgia.

5. Joseph Haydn's head. For nearly 60 years the head of the Austrian composer was stored in a cupboard in the Museum of the Vienna Academy of Music. Haydn was buried without it after two of his best friends bribed the gravedigger to let them keep it.

6. Rasputin's penis. Following his assassination by a group of Russian noblemen, his manhood was hacked off and preserved in a small velvet-lined box. The current whereabouts of this artefact are not known.

7. Sir Walter Raleigh's head. After his execution in 1618 it became the Raleigh family heirloom. His widow Elizabeth kept it for 29 years before willing it to their son Carew, who looked after it until 1666, when it went with him to his grave.

8. King Charles XII of Sweden's skull. Now on permanent public display in Stockholm,

complete with the large bullet hole which made
the exhibition possible in 1718.

9. Beethoven's hair. In 1994 two collectors paid
Sotheby's £4,000 for a four-inch-long lock of
the composer's hair, allegedly snipped by
Beethoven's dad in 1827. They said they
planned to have it DNA-tested to confirm
suspicions that the composer had African blood
and suffered from syphilis.

10. Cancerous tissue from the jaw of US President
Grover Cleveland. This resides in the Mutter
Museum of Philadelphia, which specializes in
bizarre medical curiosities, along with the B.C.
Hirot Pelvis Collection, the Sappey Collection
of mercury-filled lymphaticus, the Chevalier
Johnson Collection of foreign bodies removed
from lungs, and the joined liver of Chang and
Eng, the original Siamese Twins.

Remains of the Day:
9 Celebrity Grave Robberies
~

1. General Kitchener was sent to avenge the death of General Gordon, killed at Khartoum by the Mahdi's troops in 1885. As the Mahdi was already dead, however, Kitchener had to content himself with a spot of gratuitous desecration by blowing up the Mahdi's tomb at Omdurman and throwing his bones into the River Nile. Kitchener planned to keep the Mahdi's skull as an inkwell, but when Queen Victoria heard about Kitchener's trophy she ordered him to return it.

2. In March 1978 the body of Charlie Chaplin was stolen from its grave in Vevey, Switzerland, and held for a 600,000-franc ransom by a Pole, Roman Wardas, and a Bulgarian, Gantcho Ganev. The body-snatchers were finally arrested and Chaplin's remains were retrieved from a cornfield a few miles away. They said they needed the money to start a garage business.

3. In 1876 an American gang was apprehended while attempting to steal the remains of Abraham Lincoln. The plan was to hold them for ransom in return for the release of a convicted forger, Ben Boyd. Lincoln's coffin was subsequently embedded in steel and concrete.

4. In November 1888 the remains of the Spanish artist Francisco Goya were exhumed from the cemetery in Bordeaux, France, when he had lain for 60 years, so that they could be returned to his native country for re-burial. When the coffin was opened, however, Goya's head was missing. Its whereabouts are still unknown to this day.

5. The tomb of King William the Conqueror, situated at Caen in Normandy, France, has been raided twice. In 1562 it was desecrated by Calvinists during the French Wars of Religion, when the king's bones were left scattered around the churchyard. In 1793 the tomb was robbed by French revolutionaries. All that remains today is a stone slab marking his last known resting place.

6. In 1790 the grave of the English poet John Milton, at St Giles, Cripplegate, London, was raided by souvenir-hunters. Gravedigger Elizabeth Grant was later found to be charging visitors sixpence a time for a viewing of Milton's teeth and part of his leg.

7. The tomb of King Richard I at Westminster Abbey in London had a hole in it, through which visitors could actually touch his skull. In 1776 a schoolboy stole the king's jawbone. It was kept as a family heirloom until its eventual return to the Abbey in 1906.

8. When King Henry VIII was interred in the royal vault at Windsor Castle, a workman removed one of his finger-bones and used it to make a knife handle.

9. The hands of the Argentinian president General Juan Peron were amputated in 1987 and were held for a £5 million ransom. Fortunately, Peron had no further use for them as he had already been dead for 13 years.

10 Holy Relics

1. The personal evacuations of the Grand Llama of Tibet were considered so holy that his followers wore samples of his excrement around their necks as holy relics. His urine was also considered a powerful prophylactic, and his courtiers would mix it in their food.

2. At least 13 churches worldwide claim to own Christ's foreskin. Pope Innocent III declined to rule on which was the genuine artefact on the grounds that God alone knew the truth.

3. King Henry VII was given St George's left leg as a present.

4. Sri Lanka has a temple dedicated to one of the Buddha's teeth.

5. In the nineteenth century there were three holy navels of Christ on display in churches at Rome, at Lucques and at Chalones-sur-Marne.

6. The brain of St Peter was for several decades housed above an altar in Geneva, until it turned out to be a pumice stone.

7. St Peter's nail-clippings have surfaced in a dozen churches in Europe.

8. The body of the Welsh saint, Teilo, was at one time miraculously housed in three different locations.

9. At least 60 churches claim to be the repository of the Virgin Mary's breast milk.

10. The chamber-pot used by the late fourteenth-century saint Giovanni Columbini was renowned for its miraculous healing properties. After his death, the pot emitted a fragrant odor. A young lady suffering from a severe facial disfigurement smeared the contents of the chamber pot over her face, and was cured.

10 Uses for a Dead Person

~

1. When D.H. Lawrence died, his lover Frieda had his ashes tipped into a concrete mixer and incorporated into her new mantelpiece.

2. In 1891 French surgeon Dr Varlot developed a method of preserving corpses by covering them with a thin layer of metal (in effect, he was electroplating the dead). Dr Varlot's technique involved making the body conductive by exposing it to silver nitrate, then immersing it in a galvanic bath of copper sulphate, producing a millimeter-thick coating of copper: "a brilliant red copper finish of exceptional strength and durability."

3. In ancient Rome, where human blood was prescribed as a cure for epilepsy, epileptics hung around near the exit gates of public arenas so that they could drink the blood of slain gladiators as they were dragged out.

4. In medieval Europe it was fashionable to eat and rub into the body bits of ancient Egyptian mummy for medicinal purposes. The body parts of decomposing Egyptians were widely touted as a cure for abscesses, fractures, contusions, paralysis, migraine, epilepsy, sore throats, nausea, disorders of the liver and spleen and internal ulcers. In the early part of this century some Arab tribes were still using mummies to prevent haemorrhaging. Mummy-trafficking became a lucrative and highly organized business, starting in the Egyptian tombs and following a well-planned route to Europe. The bottom finally fell out of the mummy market in the late seventeenth century, when people found out that dealers were selling "fake" mummy made from recently murdered slaves.

5. Elizabethan medical text books recommended an alternative cure-all: powdered human skull dissolved in red wine.

6. British farmers were "processing" human corpses to create raw materials long before the Nazis

thought of it. On 18 November 1822 the *Observer* reported that the Napoleonic battle-fields of Leipzig, Austerlitz and Waterloo had been "swept alike of the bones of the hero and of the horse which he rode," and that hundreds of tons of the bones had been shipped to Yorkshire bone-grinders to make fertilizers for farmers. After the siege of Plevna in 1877 a local news-paper farming column casually reported that "30 tons of human bones, comprising 30,000 skeletons, have just landed at Bristol from Plevna."

7. German scientists involved in car safety research at the University of Heidelberg routinely use human crash dummies, including the corpses of children. Researchers in other countries have condemned the practice of smashing human cadavers into brick walls as abhorrent, but it hasn't prevented many from paying to see the results.

8. When the mistress of the nineteenth-century French novelist Eugène Sue died, she willed him

her skin, with instructions that he should bind a book with it. He did.

9. The philosopher and reformer Jeremy Bentham lamented the wasteful business of burying dead people, and suggested that every man, if properly embalmed, could be used as his own commemorative bust or statue: he called them "auto-icons." The possibilities, Bentham posited, were endless: portraits of ancestors could be replaced with actual heads, "… many generations being deposited on a few shelves or in a modest sized cupboard." When Bentham died he put his money where his mouth was by leaving instructions that his own body be dissected for the benefit of medical science, then embalmed, dressed in his own clothes, and placed in a glass case. His head had to be replaced with a wax version, however, because he had taken on an unfortunately grim expression during the embalming process. Bentham's physician, Dr Southwood Smith, kept the body until his own death in 1850, when it was presented to University College, London.

10. The size of a regulation soccer ball, roughly the same as a man's head, was arrived at by design: the first football ever used in England was the head of a dead Danish brigand.

10 All-Time Most Stressful
Funeral Experiences

~

1. In June 1988 a funeral wake was held in the Ukrainian village of Zabolotye for a man who had died of poisoning after drinking black market industrial spirit. Unwisely, the very same drink was served at the wake, resulting in 10 more deaths.

2. When William the Conqueror died in 1087 his marble coffin was found to be considerably too small for the late king. Two soldiers were required to stand on the body to squeeze it in, which they did with considerable enthusiasm, jumping up and down on it until they broke the king's back. The broken spine tore a hole in his stomach and caused it to explode with a loud bang: the stench was so overpowering that everyone present had to flee the building.

3. In 1994 a Croatian, Stanislav Kovac, was knocked down and killed by a car on a business trip to Botrop, Germany. Local undertaker

Rudolf Dauer subsequently completed a 560-mile trip from Botrop to his funeral in Zagreb, only to have to explain to bereaved relatives that he had forgotten to bring the corpse with him.

4. When Josef Stalin died in March 1953 thousands of people were trampled to death in the struggle to see his embalmed corpse lying in the state mausoleum.

5. King George IV was very badly embalmed and his body became so swollen that it almost burst through the lead lining in his coffin. The danger of explosion was averted by drilling a hole in his cask to let out some of the putrid air.

6. In 1927, when George V's wife Queen Mary attended the funeral of her brother Adolphus, the funeral procession was interrupted by the sound of her brother's body exploding noisily inside his coffin.

7. The 10th Duke of Hamilton, Alexander Douglas, outbid the British Museum when he paid £11,000 for a magnificent ancient tomb

which had originally been made for an Egyptian princess. Douglas housed it in a fabulous mausoleum at his ancestral home, Hamilton Palace, where it awaited his death. It wasn't until his death in 1852 that he was discovered to be much too tall to fit inside it. The only way they could get him in was by sawing his feet off.

8. In 1994 in Baton Rouge, US, a funeral service for a 25-year-old man was disrupted when his corpse caught fire inside the closed coffin, causing smoke to pour out of the cracks. An investigation found that the embalming fluids had spontaneously combusted.

9. In June the crematorium at the Meadow Lawn Memorial Park in San Antonio, Texas, was partially destroyed by fire. It broke out when staff began cremating a body that weighed over 300 pounds. The owner of the crematorium explained that the regular crematorium fire had raged out of control because of the fat in the body, which had caused an unusually high temperature.

10. Frederick Armstrong was convicted in 1993 of stabbing an 81-year-old preacher to death and cutting off his head before stunned onlookers, including a few police officers, at a funeral home in Baton Rouge, US. Armstrong's defence attorney appealed against the verdict on the grounds that their client was obviously insane at the time: "A rational man," reasoned Armstrong's lawyer, "does not decapitate a man in the presence of a police officer."

10 Notable Suicides

1. Zeno (336–264 BC) was the Greek who founded Stoicism, a school of philosophy characterized by impassivity and an indifference to pleasure or pain. He hanged himself at the age of 72 after falling down and wrenching his finger.

2. Socrates, Greek philosopher (470–399 BC), took the poison hemlock when he was condemned to death by his enemies.

3. Cato the Younger (95–46 BC), statesman and general, threw himself on his sword at Utica in North Africa after losing the last battle to save Rome's democracy.

4. Cleopatra VII (69–30 BC), Greek Queen of Egypt, took her own life with the help of an asp after she was militarily defeated and then rejected by Octavius.

5. Nero (AD 37–68), Emperor of Rome, cheated a Roman lynch mob by slitting his own throat.

6. Giralomo Cardano, sixteenth-century Italian mathematician and astrologer, became hugely successful after drawing up horoscopes for the crowned heads of Europe, including English king Edward VI. Cardano once boasted that he could predict his own death, down to the very hour. When the hour arrived and Cardano found himself in embarrassingly robust good health he took his own life rather than be proved wrong.

7. Robert Clive (1725–74), the man chiefly responsible for establishing British rule in India, killed himself when he was criticized for mis-government.

8. Lord Castlereagh (1769–1822) was the British foreign secretary after the Napoleonic Wars and one of the most famous statesmen in Europe. He became mentally ill and, although innocent of any wrongdoing, convinced himself that he was about to be blackmailed about a homosexual

scandal. He retired to a closet at his home and stabbed himself in the throat with a penknife.

9. Sultan Abdul Aziz of Turkey was deposed by a palace coup. Five days after his arrest he asked for a pair of scissors to trim his beard, and slashed the main arteries in both wrists.

10. Vincent van Gogh (1853–90), Dutch painter, took his own life while painting *Wheat Field with Crows*. He was depressed at having sold only one painting during his lifetime.

10 Ways to Achieve Sainthood

1. St Denis is the patron saint of syphilis and of Paris. Legend has it that after he was beheaded, St Denis walked for quite some distance carrying his head. He is not to be confused with St Fiacre, the patron saint of non-specific venereal disease, a job he combines with looking after haemorrhoid sufferers. After an altercation with a non-believer, St Fiacre sat down heavily on a rock, miraculously leaving the impression of his buttocks upon it. Christian haemorrhoid sufferers subsequently discovered that they could get relief by sitting where St Fiacre had rested.

2. St Agatha is patron saint of Malta, bell-makers, diseases of the breast, earthquakes, fire and sterility. In the third century she defended her virginity against a high-ranking Roman, was sent to prison and had her breasts cut off. These were later restored by divine intervention. She was then put in a brothel, where her virginity miraculously remained intact; burned at the

stake, but failed to ignite, then finally beheaded. Sicilians honor her feast day every year by carrying an image of her breasts through the streets.

3. The feast day of St Lawrence is 10 August. He was roasted alive on a spit, but faced his death heroically, telling his torturers: "Turn me over – I'm cooked on that side." St Lawrence is now the patron saint of rotisseurs.

4. St Apollonia is the patron saint of dentists. She achieved martyrdom after running into a mob of Egyptians, who pulled her teeth out one by one because she refused to renounce her faith.

5. Blessed William of Fenoli, whose feast day is 19 December, was a monk in the thirteenth century. One day, when he was returning from the fields with a mule, he was attacked by robbers. William defended himself by ripping off the leg of his mule, clubbing his attackers with it, then restoring the leg and continuing his journey.

6. The feast day of saints Eulampius and Eulampia, the brother and sister martyrs, is celebrated on 10 November. The couple survived being boiled in oil, moving 200 astonished onlookers to convert to Christianity on the spot. Immediately, all 200 converts were beheaded.

7. St Catherine is the patron saint of wheelwrights and philosophers and the namesake of a small firework. She lived in Alexandria, Egypt in the fourth century, and protested against the ill-treatment of Christians by the Emperor Maxentius. He had her sentenced to death on a spiked wheel. Divine providence intervened and the wheel broke, causing spikes to fly off and kill her persecutors. The emperor had her taken off the wheel and beheaded, whereupon milk flowed from her severed arteries.

8. The feast day of St Swithun is 2 July. To demonstrate his awesome self-control, he liked to sleep chastely between two beautiful virgins.

9. The feast day of St Simeon the Stylite is 5 January. The first and most famous of the "pillar hermits," he was known for his thrift, and for living on top of a column for 30 years. He demonstrated his divinity by standing on one leg for a year, and tying a rope around his waist so tightly that his lower body became putrefied and infested with maggots. He then ate the maggots, saying: "Eat what God has given you." He passed out, but was revived with a few lettuce leaves. St Simeon bowed in prayer one day and fell off his pole to his death.

10. The feast day of St Catherine of Siena is 29 April. She overcame her fear of bubonic plague victims by drinking a whole bowl of pus.

10 Royal Deaths

1. Emperor Menelik II of Ethiopia became convinced that he could cure illness by eating pages from the Bible. In 1913 he had a stroke and died while attempting to eat the entire Book of Kings.

2. Robert the Bruce, King of Scotland, died of leprosy aged 55.

3. Charles VIII of France died when, entering a tennis court in 1498, he fatally cracked his head on a low wooden beam.

4. Queen Eleanor, wife of Edward I, died of blood poisoning after sucking the pus out of her husband's septic wound.

5. King James II of Scotland died in battle in 1460 when one of his own cannons exploded and a piece of shrapnel sliced the top of his head off.

6. George II's heir Frederick, the Prince of Wales, caught a chill and died suddenly a few weeks later on 20 March 1751, aged 44. It was said that his premature death was "aggravated by an old cricketing injury."

7. Queen Caroline, wife of George IV, died of constipation, in spite of being force-fed so much castor oil that it "would have turned the stomach of a horse."

8. King Alexander I of Greece died of blood poisoning after being bitten by his pet monkey.

9. Princess Sophie of Bavaria strayed too near an unguarded gas lamp at a charity bazaar in Paris and became a human fireball, identifiable later only by her dental chart.

10. Archduke Franz Ferdinand, nephew of Emperor Franz Josef and heir to the Austrian throne, was insanely fussy about his appearance. In order to present a perfectly crease-free appearance at all times he was sewn into his suits; buttons were sewn on later for decoration only. When he was

felled by an assassin's bullet in Sarajevo on 28 June 1914 he bled to death while his aides struggled to cut him out of his clothes.

The Earth Moved for Them:
10 Post-Mortem Experiences

∿

1. The uncertainties of medieval medical science regularly produced premature burials – embarrassing for the undertaker and a pain in the arse for the victim – so it became normal to observe a three-day waiting period before the funeral took place, just to be on the safe side. It was not unknown for corpses to revive within three days but, as a Canterbury monk observed, recoveries after more than a week were a bit special. Anyone lucky enough to survive Extreme Unction, however, soon discovered that life for an ex-corpse wasn't all bier and skittles, and that there were certain strings attached. People who carried on living after receiving the final sacrament were not allowed to eat meat, to walk barefoot, or to have sex.

2. The sixteenth-century anatomist Vesalius was dissecting the body of a Spanish nobleman when the victim suddenly came round. The Don

subsequently complained to the Inquisition, and Vesalius was sentenced to death.

3. A woman freshly hanged in 1724 in Mussel-burgh, Scotland, became the center of a grisly dispute between her family and a bunch of enthusiastic anatomists. Her relatives were determined to give her a decent Christian burial; a party of medical students had other plans for the corpse, and were equally determined to get their hands on it. A bloody fight broke out over the body, which settled the argument by suddenly sitting up. The woman lived on for another 30 years with a new nickname – "Half Hangit Maggie Dickson."

4. In London in 1752 a 19-year-old traitor sat up on the dissecting table only minutes after his execution. A quick-thinking surgeon responded by clubbing him to death with a mallet.

5. The guillotine held a morbid fascination for the French medical profession, who marvelled at the speed of execution and speculated whether or not the brain would continue to function after

decapitation. Some people believed that the razor-sharp blade struck the victim so cleanly that they lost their heads before knowing anything about it, a theory fuelled by dozens of stories about victims who continued to protest after they had lost their heads. Eye-witnesses recorded that when the head of Jean Paul Marat's assassin Charlotte Corday was held up and slapped by the executioner, it showed unmistakable signs of anger. French doctors were allowed to carry out various macabre experiments on severed heads, including pinching the cheeks, sticking things up the nostrils, holding lighted candles near the eyeballs and even shouting the victim's name very loudly in the ear of the severed head. In 1880 the murderer Menesclou had the blood of a living dog pumped into his head. It was recorded that the head responded with a look of "shocked amazement." Much more recent research by Russian doctors actually gives some substance to these stories: they have found that if, for any reason, the brain is suddenly cut off from its oxygen supply, it uses an emergency system which keeps the victim conscious for several minutes.

6. The operatic composer Giacomo Mayerbeer, who lived with a constant fear of premature burial, arranged to have bells tied to his extremities so that any movement in his coffin would make a noise. To date, however, Mayerbeer has continued to decompose quietly without any outward sign of life.

7. A nineteenth-century German missionary, Reverend Schwartz, was revived by the sound of his favorite hymn being played at his funeral. Mourners were amazed to hear the voice of the prematurely buried priest from within the coffin, joining in the singing.

8. During a freak August heatwave in Romania in 1994, which brought two consecutive days of temperatures in the 100s, mortuary attendants reported incidents of recently deceased persons exploding.

9. In 1994 a Brooklyn undertaker named Harold Plinburg was taken aback when the corpse he was embalming suddenly emerged from a deep coma and gave him a severe beating. "None of my

friends in the funeral business has ever had anything like this happen," Harold observed later from his hospital bed.

10. A Spanish woman, Micaela Velasco, was being prepared for burial in her home town of Zamora in September 1996 when her lips suddenly moved. "We all had this sensation of total shock," said undertaker Francisco Heredero, "then we found she really was alive." She was subsequently examined by a doctor who declared her "as fit as a lady of her age can be." Mrs Velasco was 101 years old.

10 Original Observations made by Condemned Men

~

1. "At least I'll get some high-class education." – US murderer John W. Deering, facing the firing squad, after willing his body to the University of Utah.

2. "Pretty soon you're going to see a baked Appel." – George Appel, murderer of puns and of a New York policeman, as he was strapped into the electric chair in 1928.

3. "I am Jesus Christ." – Aaron Mitchell, cop-killer, awaiting death by gassing at San Quentin in 1967.

4. "Will that gas bother my asthma?" – Luis José Monge, at Colorado State Prison in 1967, awaiting death by gassing for the murders of his wife and three children.

5. "Warden, I'd like a little bicarb because I'm afraid I'm going to get gas in my stomach right now." –

Charles de la Roi, sentenced to death by lethal gas in 1946 in California for the murder of a fellow prison inmate, bidding for the George Appel Worst Death Chamber Pun Award of 1946.

6. "Hurry it up, you Hoosier bastard. I could hang a dozen men while you're fooling around." – mass-murderer Carl Panzram, awaiting the gallows at Leavenworth prison in 1930.

7. "Just our luck ... we haven't even got a decent day for it." – Frank Negran to his fellow murderer Alex Carrion as they awaited execution at Sing Sing in 1933.

8. "Damned if I care what you read." – murderer Alan Adam, on being informed by the sheriff of Northampton, Massachusetts in 1881 that he was going to read aloud the execution warrant before Adam was hanged.

9. "Are you sure this thing is safe?" – the Rugeley poisoner Dr William Palmer, as he was escorted

to the gallows trap door in 1855, after killing 14 people.

10. "I want to make a complaint ... the soup I had for supper tonight was too hot." – murderer Charles Fithina before his electrocution in New Jersey.

10 Most Optimistic Defences in a Criminal Law Court
~

1. Diana Smith from Kinsey, Alabama, pleaded guilty in December 1993 to tampering with a man's grave. The court heard that the 37-year-old woman had been charged with causing the man's death in 1990. She was merely digging up the casket in order to prove that he was faking it.

2. Mexican sisters Delfina and Maria Gonzalez were arrested and charged with murder in 1964 when police found the remains of at least 80 girls on the premises of their brothel. When asked for an explanation, one of the sisters volunteered: "Maybe the food didn't agree with them."

3. A court in Prince William County, Virginia, dropped charges of rape and sodomy against a 45-year-old schizophrenic after accepting evidence that one of the victim's multiple personalities had consented to have sex with one of the rapist's multiple personalities. The prose-

cution heard that the two had previously met in group therapy, and that many of their "different selves" had fallen in love and even talked of marriage.

4. In 1996 convicted Chicago paedophile Robert Ellison, 65, asked a judge for the immediate return of his child sex videos. He argued that he would surely molest more children if he could not relieve his urges through pornography. The judge opted to achieve a similar result by locking Ellison up.

5. Thirty-year-old Frederick Treesh was one of three men detained for terrorizing the Great Lakes area in North America with a series of spree killings during the summer of 1994. Treesh complained later: "Other than the two we killed, the two we wounded, the woman we pistol-whipped, and the light bulbs we stuck in people's mouths, we didn't really hurt anybody."

6. Lawyers acting for Seattle death row inmate Mitchell Rupe appealed against his hanging because it would constitute "cruel and unusual

punishment." They argued that 19-stone, 3-pound Rupe would be instantly decapitated by the pressure of his weight on the rope. The appeal failed and Rupe swung on 11 July 1994.

7. In 1996 in Providence, US, Anthony St Laurent admitted taking part in organized crime. On receiving a 10-month prison sentence, he informed the court that he was in point of fact innocent, and had only entered a guilty plea because an illness requiring 40–50 enemas a day would have made it difficult for him to sit through a very long trial.

8. In 1995 Baltimore police arrested Saladin Ishmael Taylor, 34, for the murder of a neighbor. A woman's body had been found lying next to a one-inch piece of Taylor's tongue, which had apparently been bitten off by the victim in their struggle. At his trial Taylor lisped that he had no knowledge of the murder. He admitted that he had recently lost part of his tongue in a street accident, but had no idea how it had ended up beside the woman's body.

9. Israel Zinhanga, 28, told a Zimbabwe court in 1996 that he had sex with a cow because he was afraid of contracting AIDS from a human partner.

10. In 1996 the US Supreme Court rejected the appeal of a convicted Arizona drug-user, who claimed he did not receive a fair trial because there were no fat people on the jury.

10 Most Bungled Executions

1. The most prolonged execution in French history occurred in 1626, when Count Henri de Chalais was condemned to death for his part in a royal assassination plot. When it was time for the count to be publicly beheaded with a sword, the regular executioner couldn't be found and an inexperienced replacement had to be drafted in at the last minute. The count's head was hacked off by the stand-in on the 29th stroke: he was still breathing at the 20th.

2. James Scott, the Duke of Monmouth and first-born illegitimate son of Charles II, was victim of Tower Hill's messiest execution on 15 July 1685. Although the handsome and popular duke complained loudly that the axeman's blade appeared to be very blunt, no one took much notice. In the event it was the fifth blow which finally severed his head from his shoulders just before he had a chance to say "I told you so." The crowd was appalled and the axeman narrowly escaped a lynching. It was belatedly discovered

that the duke, although a person of great historical importance, had never actually had his portrait painted for posterity. His head was duly sewn back on, the joins covered up, and his portrait taken. He now hangs in the National Portrait Gallery.

3. In 1740 a 17-year-old rapist named William Duel was hanged to death, but emerged from a deep coma to find that his body had been donated to science and a surgeon's knife was already slicing into his stomach. Duel survived and his death sentence was subsequently commuted to transportation for life.

4. Two men have survived three hangings apiece. Murderer Joseph Samuels was reprieved in 1803 after the rope broke twice on the first and second attempts, and the trapdoor failed to open on the third. A trapdoor mechanism also saved the life of convicted murderer John Lee in 1884. Even though it worked every time it was tested, it failed to open three times in the space of seven minutes. Lee was let off with life imprisonment.

5. America's most horribly bungled execution by electric chair was also one of the earliest. William Taylor was condemned to death in 1893 for killing a fellow inmate in Auburn Prison. As the first electric charge surged through his body, his legs went into spasm and tore the chair apart by his ankle strappings. The charge was switched off while running repairs were made to the chair. The switch was thrown again, but this time there was no current because the generator had burned out. Taylor was removed from the chair and given morphine in an attempt to deaden any pain he may have felt. By the time the power had been restored, Taylor was already dead; nevertheless, it was decided that the law required an electrocution, so he was strapped back into the chair and the current was passed through him for another 30 seconds.

6. In 1903 a young American, Frederick van Wormer, was sent to the electric chair for the murder of his uncle. Van Wormer was duly electrocuted and pronounced dead. In the autopsy room, as he was about to go under the scalpel, Van Wormer's eye was seen to flicker, and

he moved a hand. The prison doctor was summoned, and confirmed that two full charges of current had failed to kill the prisoner. Van Wormer was carried back to the chair and several more currents were passed through him until his death was beyond dispute.

7. Murderer James Bullen was sent to the electric chair at Sing Sing in 1932. He recovered on the way to the cemetery, leaped out of the coffin and ran off. Unfortunately for Bullen he was caught and sent back to the chair.

8. The American cannibal and child-killer Albert Fish went to the electric chair at Sing Sing in 1936. The first electric charge failed, allegedly short-circuited by dozens of needles the old man had inserted into his own body. Doctors discovered a total of 29 needles in his genitals.

9. The electrocution of John Evans in Alabama state prison in 1983 required three surges of 1,900 volts each over a period of 14 minutes to finish him off. Eye-witnesses related that they saw Evans struggling for breath as smoke began

to pour from the electrodes on his head and one of his legs. The autopsy on Evans's body revealed that he had endured fourth- and second-degree burns while he was still alive.

10. When 34-year-old American rubbish-van driver Billy White was executed in April 1992 by lethal injection in Huntsville prison, medical attendants spent 40 minutes trying to locate a vein, and it took another nine minutes for him to die.

10 Most Inspired Murder Motives

1. In 1979 two Brazilians, Waldir de Souza and Maria de Conceicao, murdered six children in Cantigulo, including a two-year-old boy. They later confessed that the killings were ritual sacrifices to ensure success in their new cement business.

2. François Gueneron was shot dead by his wife in 1995 because she could no longer tolerate his habitual flatulence. According to Mrs Catherine Gueneron, her husband, a 44-year-old French construction site manager, broke wind morning, noon and night for eight years. He finally received a pistol bullet in the chest from 35-year-old Catherine after breaking wind in her face in bed. She told Marseilles judge Gilbert St Jacques: "I just snapped."

3. In 1993 a 36-year-old man from Peking, Ge Yunbao, admitted beating a six-year-old schoolboy to death and then leaving the child's severed head on a bus. Yunbao explained that he was annoyed at being passed over for promotion.

4. In October 1987 a Chinese pig-farmer, Chen Bohong of Liuzhou, was busy slaughtering a pig when he was interrupted by taxman Sun Taichang, who presented him with a bill. Chen was so irritated by the interruption that he stopped what he was doing and killed the taxman, instead.

5. The sensitive Russian Czar Paul, who was snub-nosed and bald, had a soldier scourged to death for referring to him as "baldy." The czar later had the words "snub-nosed" and "bald" banned on pain of death.

6. During the world population conference held in Cairo in 1994, the Egyptian newspaper *Al-Wajd* reported that a delegate had stabbed his wife to death because she refused go to bed with him.

7. A Liberian general, Gray Allison, was sentenced to death in August 1989 for the murder of a policeman. He explained that he needed the policeman's blood to perform a magic rite which would overthrow Liberia's dictator Samuel Doe.

8. Self-styled emperor of the former Central African Republic Jean Bokassa had 200 schoolchildren beaten to death by his imperial guard in the 1970s. Their crime was failure to comply with school uniform regulations.

9. In March 1984 a 16-year-old Malaysian boy was beheaded by a Chinese man in Kuala Lumpur, as a human sacrifice in an attempt to win the state lottery. The murder was in vain: in the event, it was a roll-over week.

10. In September 1994 in Messina, Italy, a patient who was being treated for paranoia shot his psychiatrist. The murderer commented later: "He never liked me."

10 Capital Oddities

~

1. When murderer Albert Clozza was sent to the electric chair in Virginia, in 1991, the surge of current caused his eyeballs to pop out onto his cheeks.

2. The biggest ever mass execution in US history occurred on Boxing Day, 1862. The US army hanged 38 Sioux warriors for their part in the massacre of 800 settlers.

3. The details of precisely what the Holy Inquisition could and could not do to extract a confession were spelt out in *The Book of Death*, which was on display in the Casa Santa in Rome until the nineteenth century. There is no record of an Inquisition acquittal. The accused was not told what he or she was charged with, and was actually forbidden to ask, nor was anyone permitted a defence council or allowed to call defence witnesses.

4. Although common criminals were hanged in England in the sixteenth century, heretics were burned at the stake, so that the flames could cleanse their souls. Lucky victims were allowed to hang a small bag of gunpowder around their necks to speed death.

5. In Britain witches were never burned to death, as they often were abroad. There were other crimes for which a woman could be burned at the stake: petty treason or forgery, for example. The last female to be judicially burned to death in Britain was a woman named Murphy, convicted with a gang of forgers in London in 1789. The male members of the gang were simply hanged. The law was repealed the following year.

6. The authorized method of execution during the reign of the Roman emperor Tiberius was strangulation. There was also a law which forbade the strangling of virgins, but the resourceful Tiberius found a loophole: he ordered that virgins should first be defiled by the executioner.

7. When California's notorious San Quintin gas chamber was installed in the 1930s it was tested on live pigs. The city authorities were so proud of their "humane" new system that, in a desperately miscalculated exercise in public relations, they invited newspaper reporters to witness their first disposal of a human being. The reporters were appalled by what they saw: one described it as "more savage than being hanged, drawn and quartered."

8. A novel variation on hanging, involving a large counterweight which broke the criminal's neck by flinging the victim 12 feet in the air, was widely practised in the US in the early part of the twentieth century.

9. In May 1994 a prison in Varner, Arkansas, began a policy of executing two death row inmates at a time, because multiple executions saved money on overtime pay for employees, and were "less stressful." A prison official explained: "Nobody wants to get up in the morning and go kill somebody."

10. The longest anyone has ever survived on death row is 34 years. The Kentuckian Henry Anderson was convicted for murder in 1958 and sentenced to death in 1960. Although the state death penalty law was repealed in 1972, Anderson refused to have his sentence commuted because he said it would be an admission of guilt. In April 1994, aged 79, he died of cancer at the Kentucky State Reformatory.

10 Gruesome Collectibles

1. The fridge in which serial killer Jeffrey Dahmer, "the Milwaukee Cannibal," stored his victims' skulls was auctioned in 1996 to settle claims made by the families of some of his victims. Dahmer was beaten to death in prison in November 1994 while serving life for the sexual assault and murder of 17 young men and boys.

2. The stuffed carcass of Toto, the dog who starred with Judy Garland in the 1939 film *Wizard of Oz*, fetched £2,300 at auction in 1996.

3. In 1992 the blood-stained toe tag from the corpse of Lee Harvey Oswald, together with a lock of his hair, were auctioned in New York. The items were allegedly removed from Oswald by the ambulance driver as he drove him to the Dallas morgue.

4. A toilet seat allegedly belonging to Adolf Hitler was put up for auction in Los Angeles, California, in 1968. The seller, Guy Harris, a former American fighter pilot, claimed he rescued it from Hitler's bunker in 1945 – the only item he could find that had not already been scavenged by Russian troops.

5. The legendary bank robbers Bonnie and Clyde were enjoying bacon and tomato sandwiches in their car when they were ambushed by a posse of patrolmen and perforated by 77 bullets, splattering bits of brain all over the upholstery. The car and its contents were swooped on by local trophy-hunters, who even cut off locks of Bonnie Parker's hair. One man was apprehended by a coroner as he was attempting to saw off one of Clyde Barrow's ears.

6. The surgeon John Hunter, the unrivalled expert of eighteenth-century anatomy, was a tireless collector of anatomical artefacts, including embalmed foetuses, corpses and human and

animal skeletons. Over a period of 30 years he amassed about 65,000 items. His uncomplaining wife Anne is said to have registered a protest only once, and that was when he brought home a stuffed giraffe which was too tall to fit inside his house. Hunter shortened it by hacking the legs off below the knee, and placed it in his hall. When he died he bequeathed the lot to the Company of Surgeons in London. In May 1941 the building in Lincoln's Inn took a direct hit from a German bomber, and now only 3,600 specimens remain.

7. Lincoln's Inn was also the home of the finest collection of bladder stones ever assembled by one man. It was the pride and joy of the surgeon Sir Henry Thompson, urologist to the crowned heads of Europe. When Sir Henry died he bequeathed all 1,000 of his bladder stones, including a couple removed from Leopold I King of the Belgians and the French emperor Napoleon III, to the Royal College of Surgeons in London.

8. The world's most collectible piece of human ordure is a nine-inch stool known as the Lloyds Bank Turd. The unique Viking turd, so called because it was found in an archaeological dig under a Lloyds bank, is insured for £20,000. It is highly valued because of its near perfect condition – a rarity amongst 1,000-year-old turds.

9. Ron Sherwin of St Ives, Cornwall, has the world's only known collection of airline sick bags.

10. The wealthy nineteenth-century naturalist and explorer Charles Waterton was noted for anti-social behavior, which earned him affectionate respect as one of England's great eccentrics. Waterton loved to exhibit his prized collection of stuffed animals around his home, but found orthodox taxidermy too boring. He kept himself amused by grafting parts of different animals onto each other, and once surprised his dinner guests by displaying the partially dissected corpse of a gorilla on his dining table.

10 Creative Applications for
Formaldehyde

~

1. Dr Honoré Fragonard, eighteenth-century
anatomist and cousin of the French master Jean-
Honoré Fragonard who was famous for his
paintings of landscapes and rosy-cheeked
cherubs, made sculptures from human and
animal cadavers. His pieces, carefully skinned,
preserved in formaldehyde and posed, are now on
public view in the Fragonard Museum, which
comprises three rooms of the National Veteri-
nary School in Maisons-Alfort, on the eastern
outskirts of Paris. Fragonard set up the museum
himself in 1766, at the school where he worked
as a teacher. The school authorities, upset by
their employee's nauseating hobby, fired Fragonard in 1771, but decided to keep the museum.
Fragonard went on to enjoy a strange celebrity
status among members of the French aristocracy,
who liked to keep curious objects in their homes.
By the time the anatomist died in 1799, aged
66, hundreds of his sculptures were being used to
break the ice at the very best dinner parties.

2. By the time Eva Peron died of cancer in 1952 an eminent pathologist had been on stand-by for a fortnight to embalm her. With Eva barely dead he quickly filled her veins with alcohol, then glycerine, which kept her organs intact and made her skin appear almost translucent. Her funeral turned into a riot: as two million Argentinians filed past her coffin, seven people were crushed to death. Eva's husband Juan planned to have her housed in a giant new mausoleum, but he was forced to flee the country, and the body went missing for several years. In 1971 Juan and Eva were touchingly re-united. According to an eye-witness, Eva's corpse was ever-present at the Peron family dinner table along with Juan and his new wife Isabel.

3. Damien Hirst's Turner Prize-winning 1994 show at the Serpentine Gallery in London featured his famous animal exhibits, including Away from the Flock, a lamb embalmed in a glass case. Previous works include Mother and Child Divided comprising a dead cow and calf bisected in formaldehyde in a glass case, and a cow's head

being devoured by maggots, a piece which had to be replaced every 36 hours with a new head.

4.   The famous duellist Brian Maguire was a descendant of the ancient Fermanagh family and an officer in the East India Company. When his son George died aged 12 in 1830, Maguire decided to craft a permanent and cherished keepsake: he embalmed the boy himself and kept him in a glass case which he carried with him everywhere, until his own death five years later, of a heart attack.

5.   When Enrico Caruso died in 1921 the great Italian opera singer was laid to rest on show in a glass coffin, allowing hordes of fans to ogle at his corpse for the next five years. Five years and several new suits later, his widow decided to give him a more dignified resting place: in a private tomb.

6. Because of a fault in the embalming process, the body of Chairman Mao is shrinking at a steady rate of about 5 per cent a year. The official line given by the mausoleum director is that this is merely an optical illusion caused by the curious lighting effects in the hall which contains his corpse.

7. Ancient Egyptians didn't always bury their dead relatives after their bodies had been mummified. Families often observed the grisly ritual of keeping the body at home with them so that it could be present at meal times; some were kept above ground for several years. There was another reason for this practice: at the risk of ruining appetites and frightening the children, the mummified bodies of dead relatives were valuable assets, which could be used to guarantee loans: i.e. you could borrow money on the surety of your stiff mother, father, brother or child. Anyone who failed to discharge a debt would be refused a burial of their own.

8. When Bonnie Parker and Clyde Barrow were ambushed in their car and shot to death, their bodies were placed in a Louisiana undertaker's parlor, which was the rear room of a furniture store. The crowds who turned out to see the outlaws were so uncontrollable that the undertaker had to squirt embalming fluid on them to keep them back.

9. Most Russians are prepared to stand in line for hours only for something edible, but Vladimir Ilyich Lenin continues to be a crowd-puller in his new mausoleum at St Petersburg, although neither his reputation nor the queues are quite what they were. Lenin may have been a poor conversationalist since 1924, but the world's most famous embalmee has managed to get through several dozen new suits. Under his blue acrylic tailored three-piece, the father of communism also wears a rubber wetsuit, into which is poured the solution which keeps him from falling apart. Twice a week the parts that show – his hands and face – are painted with fresh embalming fluid, and every 18 months the

whole body is lifted out and given a thoroughly good soaking. Every four years a bit of Lenin is scraped off, placed under a microscope and examined for signs of deterioration. About 60 per cent of his body is now made of wax, including his ears: the original pickling wasn't done properly and bits of him have "gone off" since. He also sports a growth of fungus around his neck and the back of his head, which definitely wasn't there when he led the Bolsheviks to power in 1917. When communism was still popular Lenin had to be refrigerated with equipment from a German fish-freezing plant to stop him melting in the body-heat of visiting tourists.

10. When united Italy's first monarch, Victor Emmanuel II, died, Rome's daily paper *Opinione* carried a "live" eye-witness report of the deceased king as he lay in state: "He lies with his face turned slightly to the left. His eyes are closed and his appearance, maintaining a certain look of pride, has taken on an aspect of calm which is enhanced by his natural pallidness. At 7 pm this evening the embalming of the royal corpse will

begin." The newspaper went on to assure its readers that the embalming process would guarantee that: "the mortal remains of the appearance of our beloved sovereign will be conserved for the benefit of posterity." This confidence was misplaced: owing to a fault in the embalming process the old king very quickly decomposed in his new general's uniform, forcing onlookers to flee with handkerchiefs covering their noses.

10 Last Words

❦

1. "I don't know." – Pierre Abelard, philosopher, 1142.

2. "Wait a minute ..." – Pope Alexander VI, Borgia, 1503.

3. "Monks. monks, monks." – King Henry VIII, 1547.

4. "Strike, man!" – Sir Walter Raleigh (to his executioner), 1618.

5. "Am I still alive?" – Julie de Lespinasse, 1776.

6. "Enough." – Immanuel Kant, 1804.

7. "Get out." – Karl Marx, 1883.

8. "Bugger Bognor." – King George V, 1936.

9. "I am Heinrich Himmler." – Heinrich Himmler, 1945.

10. "I'm all right." – H.G. Wells, 1946.

Chapter 5

MAD, BAD AND DANGEROUS
TO KNOW

10 Zealous Officials

1. In 1994 the regulatory authority for funeral parlours in Massachusetts suspended the licence of undertaker Robert Miller for two years. They were acting upon complaints that he had dug up the remains of two cremated bodies because relatives of the deceased failed to pay their funeral bills promptly.

2. In January 1994 in Riga, Latvia, five local bus inspectors beat a 33-year-old man named Smits to death for failing to produce a valid bus ticket.

3. In 1994 Los Angeles city officials ordered a strip club owner to remove the stage upon which nude dancers performed. The authorities ruled that the stage was not wheelchair-accessible for disabled nude dancers, although they admitted that no such dancers had yet come forward.

4. In 1996, in preparation for the first death-row hanging in 50 years — that of William Bailey — officials at the Delaware Correctional Centre fixed non-skid safety strips to each of the 23 steps leading to the outdoor gallows.

5. In February 1994 the Philadelphian state weights and measures officials served notice of a violation on topless dancer Crystal Storm. The officials had ascertained that Miss Storm's bust measurement was only 50 inches, and not her advertised measurement of "127," which Miss Storm later claimed was in centimeters.

6. In 1992 the South Carolina social services department sent a letter addressed to a recently deceased person: "Your food stamps will be stopped effective March 1992 because we received notice that you passed away. May God bless you. You may re-apply if there is a change in your circumstances."

7. When the city of Kirtipor in Ceylon fell to the King of Ghorka in 1770, the victorious king ordered an accurate census of the population. His officials followed his order by amputating the noses of the entire population, then counting them.

8. In February 1996 a US coroner complained that ambulance drivers were deliberately delivering obviously deceased people to hospital so that they could bill the county for the fare. Supporting his claim, he cited the case of a recent shotgun suicide victim who was rushed to hospital even though the blast was so effective that it blew both eyeballs out of their sockets.

9. In the nineteenth century, Indian tax collectors persuaded defaulters to pay up by forcing them to drink buffalo milk laced with salt until the victim was half-dead with diarrhoea.

10. In 1988 a US tax court considered the case of Cynthia Hess, who worked under her stage name "Chesty Love" in the US state of Indiana, and her claim of a $2,088 tax deduction on her breasts against depreciation on the surgical implants that boosted her bust to size 56FF. Officials subsequently ruled that the implants were so freakishly large – they weighed about 10 pounds apiece – that Ms Hess's breasts were clearly wholly for business use, because she couldn't possibly derive any personal benefit from them.

10 Royal Soubriquets

1. Constantine the Copronymous, Byzantine Emperor. So-named because at his christening in 718 the baby Constantine defecated in the baptismal font.

2. Pepin the Hunchback, ninth-century Frankish prince.

3. Alfonso the Fat, thirteenth-century king of Portugal.

4. Pedro the Cruel, fourteenth-century king of Castile.

5. Ethelred the Unready, king of England. At his christening, baby Ethelred urinated in the font and defiled the holy water. This was taken as an unlucky omen that he would be unfit to rule.

6. Stephen the Fop, fourteenth-century Bavarian duke.

7. Louis the Fat, Grand Dauphin, son of King Louis XIV of France.

8. Otto the Idle, king of Prussia. Never set foot in his homeland, and once attempted to sell it.

9. Henry the Impotent, prince of Castile. So-named for his inability to consummate his marriage with his wife, due to a deformity of his foreskin.

10. Selim the Grim, sultan of Turkey.

10 Milestones in the History of New Laddism

~

1. 323 BC: Alexander the Great conquers most of the known world, then drops dead, during a drinking contest, aged 32.

2. AD 211: The young Roman emperor Heliogabalus has a couple of palace dinner guests suffocated in rose petals for a laugh.

3. 1544: The young Ivan the Terrible amuses himself by throwing live dogs off the Kremlin roof "to observe their pain."

4. 1561: King Philip II of Spain's son and heir Don Carlos, a mentally retarded psychopath who is eventually disinherited, locked up and quietly done away with, has young girls whipped for his enjoyment, has animals roasted alive while he watches, and murders at least six men for some real or imagined slight against him. When he is dissatisfied with a pair of boots made for him, he has them cut into pieces and forces the cobbler to eat them. On another occasion, when some water

is inadvertently emptied from a house balcony and splashes near him, he has the occupants executed.

5. 1712: Peter the Great's son Alexis travels to Dresden to marry a German princess. The Elector of Hanover Ernst August notes that the tsarevitch shits in his bedroom and wipes his backside with the curtains.

6. 1741: The Comte de Charolais, cousin of French king Louis XV, orders his coachman to run over any monks he encounters on the road, and shoots a man he sees working on a roof, for the hell of it. The king pardons his psychopathic cousin with the warning: "Let it be understood, I will similarly pardon anyone who shoots you."

7. 1793: The Russian Grand Duke Constantine, a grandson of Catherine the Great, amuses himself by kicking Hussars to death and firing live rats from cannon.

8. 1813: Twenty-five-year-old Lord Byron impregnates his half-sister Augusta.

9. 1828: King Miguel of Portugal tosses live piglets into the air and catches them on the point of his sword.

10. 1909: Prince George of Serbia, eldest son and heir of King Peter I, is removed from the line of succession after kicking his valet to death.

10 Women Behaving Badly

~

1. In 1603, as 30,000 Londoners were dying of the plague, Queen Elizabeth I responded to the national crisis by fleeing with her court to Windsor Castle, where she had a gallows set up, with the promise that she would hang anyone who tried to follow her.

2. Queen Henrietta, wife of the Belgian king Leopold II, kept a pet llama which she taught to spit in the face of anyone who stroked it.

3. The Russian empress Anne was fond of making up interesting new punishments to fit the crime. When she decided that two overweight noble-women were guilty of being greedy, she had them force-fed huge amounts of pastries until they almost choked to death on their own vomit. Few complained about the treatment: the empress always had their tongues pulled out first.

4. Empress Catherine I of Russia was a chronic alcoholic who shuffled through most of her reign

in a drunken haze. She once survived an assassination attempt, too drunk to realize that anything had happened. While she was reviewing a Guards regiment, a bullet flew past her and killed an innocent bystander. The empress moved on without flinching.

5. Messalina, wife of the Roman emperor Claudius, claimed an all-time record for marital infidelity when she slept with 25 men in 24 hours. She often left the imperial palace at night in disguise and went to work at a local brothel, under the name Lycisca.

6. Queen Cleopatra tested the efficacy of her poisons by feeding them to her slaves.

7. Elizabeth de B'athory, the deranged late sixteenth- and seventeenth-century lesbian Hungarian countess, believed she could reverse the ageing process by bathing in warm virgins' blood. In 1612, acting on countless rumors about her activities, troops stormed her castle and caught her literally red-handed. All her

servants were executed and burned. The countess herself was sealed in her bedroom and left to die.

8. The Russian empress Elizabeth was extremely vain. She would not tolerate competition and no one else at court was ever allowed to wear her favorite color, pink. The empress was naturally fair-haired, but had her hair dyed black to conform with the fashion of the day; when the fashion changed and she wanted to revert to blonde, she was unable to remove the dye from her hair and, in a fit of temper, shaved it all off. All her ladies-in-waiting were duly obliged to have their heads shaved, too.

9. Queen Maria Luisa of Spain had 24 childbirths and miscarriages, none of them attributable to her husband King Charles IV, who went through his entire marriage in blissful ignorance of his wife's countless adulterous relationships. The half-wit king even promoted his wife's regular lover — a sausage merchant half her age — to first minister of Spain.

10. Manuela, the widowed mother-in-law of France's emperor Louis Napoleon, was a major embarrassment to the French royal family. After a sex scandal had ended her career as head of the household to Queen Isabella of Spain, Manuela took to selling sexual favors to British ministers visiting Madrid. The main source of gossip, however, were the country house orgies she regularly attended with young men half her age. She and several other middle-aged aristocratic women kidnapped young men who took their fancy and forced the captives to crawl around the floor naked on all fours, while the women straddled their backs and pretended they were knights jousting.

10 Failed Suicides

1. King Mithridates VI, who ruled in Asia Minor in the first century BC, deliberately took small doses of poison in the hope that he could build up enough resistance to survive a possible assassination by poisoning. He finally got an opportunity to test his theory in 63 BC. In an attempt to take his own life rather than fall into the hands of the invading Romans, he tried to poison himself. His body was so full of toxins that the poison had no effect at all, and the king had to order a slave to finish him off with his sword: hence the term "mithridate," meaning antidote.

2. In 1814 the defeated Napoleon abdicated and swallowed a phial of opium he had carried about him for two years. It left him alive but screaming with stomach cramps. He had planned to blow his brains out, but his valet had emptied the powder from the brace of pistols he always kept by his bed. Napoleon's attempted suicide was kept secret until 1933.

3. In March 1996 a Taiwanese couple, Huang Pin-jen, 27, and Chang Shu-mei, 26, of Kaohsiung, opted for a suicide pact when their parents refused to bless their recent marriage. The couple survived three suicide attempts, including driving their car off a cliff and a double hanging. Finally, after they survived a leap (from the top of a 12-story building) with multiple fractures (they landed on a roof), the in-laws promised to reconsider.

4. In 1994 financial problems caused seven members of a family from Council Bluffs, Iowa, aged between 10 and 71, to climb into the family car intent upon suicide. The driver engineered a deliberate crash, which injured the three occupants of the other car, but left him and his seven suicidal passengers completely unhurt.

5. In Manila in 1994, depressed Rogelio Aparicio, 46, pulled out a gun on the steps of his local police station and fired two shots at his own head, missing completely both times.

6. Robert, Lord Clive "of India" (1725–74) twice failed to shoot himself in 1744. After the second attempt he declared: "It appears I am destined for something. I will live."

7. In 1993 *The Lancet* reported that an Englishman attempting suicide had been rescued after spending more than an hour inhaling automobile exhaust fumes. The medical journal explained that the man's bid to end his life had been thwarted by the relatively low carbon monoxide content of the exhaust, due to new European Community catalytic converter standards.

8. Empress Eugenie, wife of the French emperor Louis Napoleon III, attempted suicide by breaking off the heads of phosphorous matchsticks and then dissolving them in milk.

9. Classical composer Hugo Wolf (1860–1903) was institutionalized after attempting to drown himself.

10. In 1995 in Iola, Kansas, a 51-year-old prison inmate, Richard Barber, tried to kill himself by secretly hoarding enough dental floss to wrap around his neck and then leaping off a ledge. He succeeded only in badly cutting his neck. Barber was serving time for murdering a dentist.

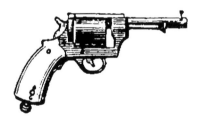

10 Phobias of the Famous

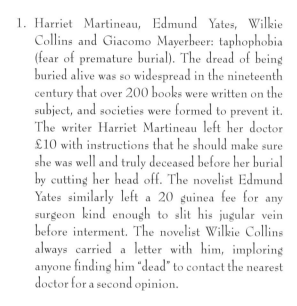

1. Harriet Martineau, Edmund Yates, Wilkie Collins and Giacomo Mayerbeer: taphophobia (fear of premature burial). The dread of being buried alive was so widespread in the nineteenth century that over 200 books were written on the subject, and societies were formed to prevent it. The writer Harriet Martineau left her doctor £10 with instructions that he should make sure she was well and truly deceased before her burial by cutting her head off. The novelist Edmund Yates similarly left a 20 guinea fee for any surgeon kind enough to slit his jugular vein before interment. The novelist Wilkie Collins always carried a letter with him, imploring anyone finding him "dead" to contact the nearest doctor for a second opinion.

2. Nicolae Ceaucescu and Marlene Dietrich: bacillophobia (fear of germs). The former Rumanian dictator and his wife once staged a "walk-about" for publicity purposes, which required them to

shake a few hands and kiss small children. The secret police selected a few volunteers beforehand and had them locked up for weeks and regularly disinfected in readiness for the big day. Marlene Dietrich's obsession led her to be known by Hollywood insiders as "the Queen of Ajax."

3. Natalie Wood, US actress: hydrophobia (fear of water). She drowned in 1981.

4. Sigmund Freud: siderodromophobia (fear of trains).

5. Samuel Johnson: lyssophobia (fear of insanity). Johnson often begged his wife to lock him in his room and shackle his legs because he was convinced he was going mad.

6. George Bernard Shaw: coitophobia (fear of sex). Shaw lost his virginity to an elderly widow at the age of 29. He was so shocked by the experience

that he didn't bother to try it again for another 15 years.

7. King Louis XV: cypridophobia (fear of syphilis). He took to sleeping with very young girls, aged between 14 and 19, because it reduced his chances of catching it.

8. Maximilian Robespierre: haematophobia (fear of blood). Thanks to the French Revolutionary the guillotine in the Place de la Révolution in Paris was in almost continuous use. Robespierre himself was extremely squeamish, however, and couldn't bring himself to look at the blood stains on the street cobbles.

9. Robert Schumann, German composer: metallophobia (fear of metal). He especially disliked keys.

10. Queen Christina of Sweden: entomophobia (fear of fleas). The mentally unbalanced seventeenth-century monarch had a four-inch cannon built so that she could spend most of her time firing tiny cannonballs at the fleas in her bedroom.

The Top 10 Causes of Madness in the Eighteenth Century*

~

1. Moving into a new home.

2. Squeezing a pimple.

3. Old age.

4. Childbirth.

5. The menstrual cycle.

6. Shrinkage of haemorrhoids.

7. Misuse of mercury.

8. Disappointment in love.

9. Masturbation.

10. Bloodletting.**

*As listed in the standard text on the subject of madness, written by the leading French physician Jean Esquirol.
**Particularly confusing to a medical profession which still believed bloodletting to be a cure for madness.

10 Bad Hair Days

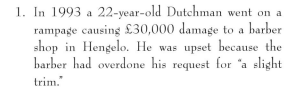

1. In 1993 a 22-year-old Dutchman went on a rampage causing £30,000 damage to a barber shop in Hengelo. He was upset because the barber had overdone his request for "a slight trim."

2. Californian hairdresser Joseph Middleton, 56, was sentenced to 60 days' community service in 1996. Middleton had masturbated with his free hand while doing his female customer's hair: at his trial the court heard that he had, in fact, been able to finish both jobs, because the customer was too frightened to object.

3. Mary Queen of Scots was bald, a secret which she hid even from many of her closest acquaintances with a thick auburn wig. The first hint that Mary was follically challenged was on the day of her execution. After she had been beheaded the executioner picked her head up by the hair to show it to the crowd, and it came away in his hand.

4. In 1994 hundreds of Uruguayans sued a local shampoo manufacturer after using the patent dandruff treatment Dander-Ban. However, none of the victims, male or female, could argue with the company's advertising claim that Dander-Ban was guaranteed to get rid of their dandruff: within hours of using the shampoo they had gone completely bald.

5. In March 1983 the Danish hair-fetishist Luigi Longhi was jailed for life after he was found guilty of kidnapping, then murdering a West German girl hitch-hiker. Longhi admitted he'd washed her hair four times before strangling her.

6. Hair from corpses was widely used in the manufacture of wigs for 300 years, although the quality of hair was nothing to write home about. The bottom fell out of the periwig business during the Great Plague of London in 1665. No one dared buy a new wig for fear that the hair had been cut off the heads of plague-infected cadavers. Samuel Pepys once recorded in his dairy that he had bought a brand new wig, but had quickly returned it to his barber in disgust

because it was full of headlice. "It vexed me cruelly," Pepys wrote, "that he should put such a thing in my hands."

7. Michael Potkul, 33, won a $400,000 malpractice award against surgeon Dominic Brandy in Pittsburgh, US in 1996. Brandy had promised Potkul that he could give him a nearly full head of hair by grabbing the hairy scalp at the back of his head and stretching it over the bald bit on top. Potkul became so depressed after six unsuccessful operations that he attempted suicide.

8. According to Ronnie Spector, singer with the 1960s US girl band The Ronettes, her famous writer/producer husband Phil always switched the light off when they went to bed so that he could remove his toupee in private. He then applied so much solvent to get rid of the glue that held it in place that for the rest of the night he had a reek that would kill a horse.

9. In Denver, David Joseph Zaba, 32, pleaded guilty to assault for pouring varnish on his wife during sex, causing her hair to fall out. The court heard

that the couple had been using food as part of their sex life for seven years: on this particular occasion Angela Zaba was expecting honey and chocolate syrup.

10. In 1994 Ernestine and John Kujan sued the New York dog-grooming salon Pet Pavilion after watching their cocker spaniel Sandy accidentally bake to death in an automatic blow dryer.

10 Facts about the Church you are least likely to hear in Sunday School

 ～

1. The Book of Esther is the only book in the Bible which neglects to mention God.

2. Although the Church frowned on adultery from the beginning, it didn't get around to banning sex with animals until the Council of Ankara in AD 314.

3. The modern confessional box was invented in the Middle Ages to help prevent women from being sexually assaulted by priests.

4. The early Christian Church held that the Virgin Mary was impregnated through her ear. Paranoia about aural sex was so widespread that the naked ear was considered sexually explicit, hence the fashion for tight-fitting wimples.

5. The Catholic Church accepts cannibalism as a justifiable means of saving one's life.

6. Onan, the son of Judah, "spilled his seed" in the Old Testament (Genesis 38:8–10), thus becoming the Bible's sole masturbator. The passage is the basis for the Church's unreserved condemnation of masturbation for centuries, and gave rise to the expression Onanism, a term for self-abuse which was still popular in Victorian times.

7. The Old Testament book Ecclesiasticus recommends clearing the stomach by throwing up before or during a big meal to make room for more food.

8. The Bible was full of lepers. It was written at a time when any skin defect, even a bad case of acne, was likely to get people branded as a leper and shunned by society. Most "lepers" were probably sufferers of syphilis. As they would also, to all intents and purposes, be written off as dead, they would have a requiem mass sung for then, as was the custom for all living lepers.

9. In the twelfth and thirteenth centuries the Church declared a holy war on cats, because they

were ambassadors of the devil. After two centuries of persecution, the cat population of Europe was decimated, and there followed an explosion in the rat population, bringing with it the Plague. The Catholic Church duly reversed its position on cats, and issued a new proclamation that anyone caught abusing a cat would be excommunicated.

10. At one time you could be excommunicated for wearing a wig.

10 Celebrity Fashion and Beauty Tips

~

1. On the day of his execution, King Charles I wore two vests.

2. In his later years, composer Gioacchino Rossini suffered from alopecia, which made him completely bald, and he took to wearing a wig. In exceptionally cold weather he wore two or three wigs simultaneously.

3. Queen Isabeau, wife of King Charles VI of France, decreed that the waistlines of all her court ladies-in-waiting should not exceed a maximum of 13 inches. In the process of meeting this requirement, a few of them starved to death.

4. Queen Anne's cousin, Lord Cornbury, the 3rd Earl of Clarendon, was governor-general of New York and New Jersey from 1701 to 1708. Cornby was a veteran British parliamentarian and a transvestite. In 1702 this large, heavily built man opened the New York Assembly

wearing a blue silk ball gown studded with diamonds, satin shoes and a fancy headdress. When Queen Anne's American subjects complained about their governor's dress code, Cornbury dismissed the locals as "stupid." It was perfectly obvious, he said, that as a representative of Her Majesty he had a duty to represent her as accurately as he could.

5. In an attempt to make himself more attractive to his girlfriend, Gala, Salvador Dali shaved his armpits until they bled and wore a perfume made of fish glue and cow dung.

6. When syphilis robbed the great sixteenth-century Danish astronomer Tycho Brahe of his nose he had an attractive artificial gold and silver version made.

7. The famous French racing driver Jean Behra (1921–59) wore a plastic right ear after losing one in a racing crash in 1955. He always carried a spare false ear in his pocket, just in case.

8. Queen Elizabeth I always carried a bag of sweets to mask her foul breath. Sugar was so expensive in Elizabethan England that black teeth were a sign of affluence. When she finally lost all her teeth, Elizabeth took to stuffing layers of cloth under her lips to fill out her face. The queen's breasts were always heavily powdered and covered in ceruse, the popular lead-based whitener which scarred and poisoned the women of northern Europe for centuries, and her veins were highlighted with blue dye. She also wore an attractive hair pomade made from a mixture of apples and puppy fat.

9. Mae West wore 10-inch heels and false nipples.

10. Following a visit to the US by Diana, Princess of Wales in 1996, the *New York Observer* reported that requests for colonic irrigation treatments had increased tenfold.

History's 10 Biggest Fashion Mistakes

~

1. See-through clothes: all the rage in Imperial Rome during the reign of Nero. The clothes exposed both the breasts and the genitals. The trouble was, noted Seneca, "our women have nothing left to reveal to their lovers in the bedroom that they have not already shown on the street."

2. The codpiece: essential fashion accessory for Renaissance man, designed to fit around the male member like the finger of a glove, and worn throughout Europe in the fifteenth century. Contemporary fashion critic Michel de Montaigne wondered: "What is the purpose of that monstrosity that we to this day have fixed to our trousers, and often, which is worse, beyond its natural size through falseness and imposture?" Probably it was originally devised to facilitate the armored knight's call to nature.

3. Flea cravats: for about 200 years, from the fourteenth century onwards, English ladies wore

special fur collars. The accessory was designed to attract fleas, thus luring them away from the rest of their clothing.

4. False eyebrows: in the eighteenth century both men and women wore sets of mouseskin eyebrows stuck on with fish glue.

5. Bound feet: the Chinese fashion for foot-binding dates from the thirteenth century and the Empress Taki. She was born with a club foot, and her courtiers took to binding their own feet in cloth to imitate her. Before very long tightly bound, deformed feet became highly desirable in Chinese women. Their husbands encouraged foot-binding because their crippled wives were less likely to run away.

6. Erection restrainers: Queen Victoria's consort Prince Albert gave his name to a form of body-piercing, once fashionable amongst Victorian gentlemen, whereby erections could be restrained by a row of small hoops.

7. Exposed genitals: until Edward VI passed a law in 1548 banning any man below the rank of lord from exposing "his privy member and buttokkes," fashion in medieval England dictated that all should expose their naked genitals below short-fitting tunics. If the genitals weren't big enough a chap could wear padded flesh-colored falsies, or braquettes.

8. Soliman's Water: the top brand name beauty lotion of the sixteenth century, applied to the skin to eliminate spots, freckles and warts. It was highly efficient, although applying a blowtorch to your face would have had similar consequences. The chief ingredient of this lotion was mercury, which burned away the outer layers of skin and corroded the flesh underneath. One side effect was that it made teeth fall out even more quickly than was usual at this time.

9. Radiation beauty treatments: one of the most popular items to be found in North American beauty parlors in the 1920s were X-ray machines, designed to remove unwanted facial and body hair. Radiation was also touted as a

cure-all for every imaginable disease: products available included radioactive toothpaste for whiter teeth and better digestion, radioactive face creams to lighten the skin and radium-laced chocolate bars. A brisk trade in radioactive patent medicines thrived well into the 1930s. One of the most popular preparations was radium water, promoted in the US as a general tonic and known as "liquid sunshine." It was responsible for the deaths of several thousand people. In 1932 Frederick Godfrey, the "well-known British Hair Specialist," was advertising a radioactive hair tonic, and as late as 1953 a company in Denver was promoting a radium-based contraceptive jelly.

10. Colored teeth: in sixteenth-century Italy the most fashionable women colored their teeth. Russian women always dyed them black.

10 Contemporary Cures for Bubonic Plague

1. Wash the victim in goat's urine.

2. Apply the entrails of a new-born puppy to the victim's forehead.

3. Drink menstrual blood.

4. Pierce your testicles.

5. Inhale fumes from a latrine.

6. Commit incest on an altar.

7. Smoke tobacco.

8. Apply dried toad to the bubo.

9. Eat the pus-filled boil of plague victims.

10. Eat a little treacle after rainfall.

The Great Unwashed: 10 Historical Stinks

~

1. Ludwig van Beethoven had such a disregard for personal cleanliness that his friends had to take away his dirty clothes and wash them while he slept.

2. The Chinese communist leader Chairman Mao decided early in his career never to take a bath or to brush his teeth – the latter on the grounds that tigers never brushed their teeth, either. He achieved an epic personal hygiene problem which grew steadily worse as the years went by. As a septuagenarian he had several young concubines rub his body down with hot towels.

3. The Bombay religious mystic Ramasubba Sitharanjan, who eschews personal hygiene as proof of his faith to his followers, claims not to have bathed, shaved or brushed his teeth in 65 years.

4. St Francis of Assisi listed personal filthiness among the insignia of piety, in line with the early teachings of the Christian Church, which held that dirtiness was next to Godliness and that bathing was an evil, ungodly vanity punishable by an eternity in hell. A fourth-century Christian pilgrim boasted that she hadn't washed her face for 18 years. St Anthony never washed his feet and St Abraham didn't wash his hands or feet for 50 years. St Sylvia never washed any part of her body except her fingertips.

5. Czar Peter the Great, renowned throughout Europe for his occasional personal hygiene, was once described as a "baptized bear." He was incredibly dirty and smelly even by eighteenth-century standards, and blissfully unaware of rudimentary table manners or even basic potty training. When the czar and his courtiers visited London, onlookers noted that they intermittently dripped pearls and lice as they walked.

6. When the Prussian King Frederick the Great grew older and more eccentric he took on a major personal hygiene problem. His clothes remained unchanged for years and he shuffled in rags around his palace, which came to resemble a vagrant's squat, ankle-deep in places in excrement provided by his pack of beloved Italian greyhounds. When he died the shirt on his back was so rotten with sweat that his valet had to dress him in one of his own shirts for the burial.

7. Louis XIV was an enthusiastic lover, but his advances were a trying time for those mistresses with a keen sense of smell. When his doctor ordered him to bathe for medical reasons, the French king tried to get out of it by pretending he had a terrible headache as soon as he became immersed in water, and he vowed never to repeat the experience again. In all he took only three baths in his lifetime, each of them under protest.

8. Genghis Khan's Mongol warriors were a superstitious bunch who believed that washing was a sacrilege. There was also a more practical reason for their lax approach to ablutions: the thick crust of dirt which covered their bodies helped them withstand temperatures as low as minus 43 degrees Fahrenheit. Khan's men used their lack of hygiene as a weapon of psychological warfare: their enemies could smell the festering Mongol hordes long before they could see them and were often paralysed with fear by the time they arrived.

9. The 11th Duke of Norfolk was renowned as one of the richest and the smelliest men in England. In his entire life the "Dirty Duke" never once voluntarily bathed: when his servants found it impossible to occupy the same room as him they used to get him blind drunk and quickly bathe him before he regained consciousness.

10. Although the French King Henri IV was known, unusually for the time, for being a stickler for changing his shirts regularly, he still went around

his court "smelling like carrion." When his fiancée, Marie de Médicis, met him for the first time, the stench almost made her faint.

Chapter 6

AD NAUSEUM

10 Historical Deformities

1. Moses was a reluctant public speaker, who described himself as "heavy of mouth." He had a major speech impediment, and probably suffered from a cleft lip and palate. In Exodus 6:12:30 Moses describes his mouth as having "uncircumcised lips."

2. Anne Boleyn had six fingers on her left hand, and three nipples. If King Henry VIII's charges against her of adultery and incest had failed he planned to use this as evidence to have her burned as a witch.

3. Marshall Talleyrand had a deformed leg, the result of being dropped by his nurse.

4. John Keats had an unusually small head.

5. Lord Byron had a club foot shaped like a cloven hoof.

6. Napoleon had only one testicle.

7. Kaiser "Bill" Wilhelm II had a stunted and withered left arm, the result of a complicated breech birth.

8. Josef Stalin's left foot had webbed toes and his left arm was noticeably shorter than his right.

9. Josef Goebbels had a club foot. His left leg was eight centimeters longer than his right. He was born with the disability, but the official version was that it was the result of a childhood illness. The possibility that one of the architects of the Nazi movement had a genetic defect didn't sit too well with the prevailing ideology.

10. According to Soviet medical reports, Adolf Hitler did indeed have only one ball.

1. In 1994 26-year-old stripper Lisa Evans filed an appeal for unfair dismissal against the owners of a nightclub where she had worked in a nude peepshow booth in Edmonton, Alberta. Management said customers had complained that the 19 stone, 4-pound stripper was difficult to fantasize over.

2. Madras train announcer Rajiv Kamir was fired in September 1996 for breaking wind over the PA system to the opening of Beethoven's Fifth. A railway spokesman noted: "It was a disgusting deviation from the timetable."

3. The fifteenth-century German emperor Wenceslas, a violent and unstable drunk, had his cook roasted on a spit when his normally exemplary meals fell below standard. On another occasion he was out hunting when he came across a passing monk and shot him dead:

Wenceslas explained that monks had better things to do than wander about in woods.

4. Exotic dancer Pamela Harrison was dismissed by the Kat Tales club in Stuart, Florida, in 1996. Fellow dancers complained that she was a health hazard because she wore her colostomy bag tucked into her G-string during her performances.

5. The French king Louis XV understood nothing about money. When he heard that the workers were starving he sympathetically sacked 80 gardeners.

6. King Gustavus I of Sweden hacked to death his royal goldsmith because he took a day off without permission.

7. In 1994 US neurosurgeon Dr Raymond Sattle was removed from his post after he left a patient

alone on the operating table with his brain exposed for half an hour, while he went out for his lunch break. The North Carolina Board of Medical Examiners heard that Dr Sattle also frequently forgot the names of his surgical instruments during operations, allowed an untrained nurse to drill holes in a patient's head, and had intravenous fluids pumped into his own veins while he was operating to help him stay on his feet.

8. Henry VIII invented a new method of execution for Richard Rosse, cook to the Bishop of Rochester, who had poisoned the soup at a formal banquet and killed 17 people over dinner. The king had him boiled to death in one of his own stockpots.

9. Forty-year-old Milton Ross was fired from his desk job in St Joseph, Montana in 1994 after a video camera recorded him urinating into the office coffee pot. The video trap was set after his colleagues noted that their morning coffee seemed "off."

10 Susan Franano, general manager of the Kansas City Symphony Orchestra, sacked oboist Ken Lawrence in 1993 after he made a "facetious response" to a complaint about him. It appears that during a rehearsal for *Nutcracker*, Lawrence had broken wind in a loud manner, "creating an overpowering smell."

10 Extraordinary Origins

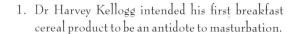

1. Dr Harvey Kellogg intended his first breakfast cereal product to be an antidote to masturbation.

2. In Britain and the US opium was originally recommended as a cure for cholera, dysentery, toothache, flatulence, the menopause and mental illness, and was once the basis for many patent baby-soothing remedies.

3. When Sir Walter Raleigh brought tobacco and potatoes back with him from the New World they received a mixed reception. It was generally agreed that spuds were a health hazard leading to scrofula, consumption, flatulence and unnatural carnal lust; tobacco, on the other hand, was quite harmless.

4. Digestive biscuits were originally made as an aid to control flatulence.

5. The first tomato ketchup was sold in the US as a patent medicine.

6. Vaseline was invented in 1859 in Brooklyn, New York, by a young chemist named Robert Chesebrough. It was to be used for dressing cuts and bruises, removing stains from furniture, polishing wood surfaces, restoring leather and preventing rust. Chesebrough also recommended a spoonful every day for good health: he ate a spoonful every morning and died aged 96.

7. Marmite was originally prescribed in the Middle East as a cure for Beri Beri. A 1951 British army medical report confirmed that Marmite was an effective treatment for scrotal dermatitis.

8. Salversan, the first effective treatment for syphilis, was invented by the admirably persistent Paul Ehrlich in 1910. It was popularly known as Treatment 606 because it was Ehrlich's 606th attempt to find a cure.

9. Atlanta pharmacist John Pemberton first stumbled across the original recipe for Coca-Cola in 1886. At the time he was working on a series of patent medicines and hair restorers, including Triplex Liver Pills, Indian Queen Hair Dye and Globe of Flower Cough Syrup.

10. Bayer, the company known for manufacturing aspirin, created Heroin as a brand name for their patent cough medicine. The exciting new wonder drug, first made in 1898 from synthesized morphine, was the subject of an intense advertizing campaign at the turn of the century. Heroin was also used to "cure" morphine addiction, to send babies with colic to sleep, and as a general pain-killer. By 1920 the streets of New York City had far fewer hacking coughs, but an estimated 300,000 heroin addicts.

10 Professions In Need of a Union

~

1. Henry VIII employed a Groom of the Stool, who was required to wipe the royal anus.

2. The ancient Egyptian pharoahs employed human fly traps, who were smeared with asses' milk and made to stand in a corner of the room.

3. The diamond company De Beers once employed security guards to undertake fingertip searches through the faeces of their fellow employees, to make sure they weren't taking their work home with them.

4. In the court of Imperial China, human wet nurses were trained to suckle the royal Pekinese puppies.

5. In 1895 a dispute over trading rights resulted in an attack by more than a thousand angry tribesmen, led by King Koko, on the British-owned Niger Company in Akassa. The native chiefs later sent a letter to Britain, addressed to

the Prince of Wales, expressing their deep regrets for having taken the law into their own hands, and especially for having eaten his employees.

6. The ancient Egyptians were martyrs to their bowels: believing that all diseases were diet-related, they binged on laxatives and purged themselves for three days at a time. The court official who supplied the enema to the pharaoh was given the title Shepherd to the Royal Anus.

7. Because the average weight of a Japanese Sumo wrestler is about 22 stone, and many of them are too fat to wipe their own backsides, novice wrestlers are expected to do it for them. Six out of every 10 novices vanish from their workplace in the first year of apprenticeship.

8. In eighteenth-century London, long before the invention of the public convenience, it was possible to make an honest living from owner-ship of a long cloak and a bucket. You simply walked the streets until you found a desperate client, then for an agreed fee wrapped the cloak

around him and looked the other way while your client relieved himself.

9. In 1911 the Japanese emperor was delayed for 20 minutes when his train jumped the points. A station master accepted responsibility and disembowelled himself.

10. The world's most difficult stand-up comic routine was performed by the eunuch dwarfs in the court of the Ottoman sultans. The dwarfs were required to keep the royal womenfolk amused while they gave birth.

You Shouldn't Have: 10 Original Gifts

~

1. In 1995 Lord Erskine of Rerrick bequeathed his testicles to the Bank of Scotland, which had declared him bankrupt, because it had "no balls."

2. At Christmas in 1888 Vincent van Gogh called at a Paris brothel known as the House of Tolerance with a present for one of the girls, whose name was Rachel, and told her "keep it and treasure it." It was his ear.

3. Moulay Ismael, the sultan of Morocco from 1672 to 1727, gave samples of his bowel movements to ladies of the court as a mark of special favor.

4. On Queen Isabel of Spain's birthday, Pope Pius IX gave her the embalmed corpse of Saint Felix.

5. Edward VII owned a golf bag made from an elephant's penis. It was a gift from an admirer, an Indian maharajah.

6. Warriors of the cannibal Brazilian Cubeo tribe always gave their wives the penis and scrotum of defeated victims. The wives were expected to eat them, and thus became fertile.

7. Pills made from the toxic metal antimony were highly esteemed in medieval times as great bowel-regulators. The pill irritated the intestinal tract, causing loose motions, and would pass through the body unharmed, enabling them to be handed down from father to son and from mother to daughter as precious family heir-looms.

8. The 1897 Sears, Roebuck & Co. mail order catalogue offered a selection of hypodermic syringe kits for shooting up heroin.

9. The most generous last will and testaments of all were left by Ecuadoran Indian endo-cannibals – i.e. cannibals who eat and are eaten by members of their own family. Their wills gave express details of which body parts were to be eaten by which lucky relative. When the will had been read, the funeral became a banquet, as the corpse

was roasted, cut into pieces and consumed by grieving relatives. The head was generally kept until it was ripe with maggots, then the brains were eaten with spices.

10. When Albert Einstein died in 1955 his body was cremated, but his brain was preserved in a glass jar. It was Albert's dying wish that his best bit should be given to science so that post-mortem analysis should shed new light on the rare gift of human genius. It didn't.

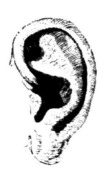

10 Odd Losses

⁓

1. In October 1993 the US Air Force confessed that it had again lost an $18 million F-16 fighter plane, because the pilot was unable to control the aircraft while using his "piddle pack" during in-flight urination. The earlier F-16 crash had been in March 1991.

2. Sixty-four-year-old widow Jean Carberry was distraught when, in October 1996, she accidentally put her husband Dennis's ashes out for the bin-men, but resolved to become reunited with him by searching through hundreds of tons of rubbish on the council tip. "I'd recognize him straight away," she explained hopefully. "He was in a green Barnardo's plastic bag ... Dennis was a bloke in a million."

3. A German whose tongue was cut off during a drunken brawl at a party in Leipzig in 1994 scoured the floor for it in the hope of having it sewn back on. The 45-year-old gave up his

search when someone commented that they had seen it eaten by a cat.

4. In 1973 the New York City Police Department admitted that they had lost about 400 pounds of heroin and cocaine, with a combined estimated street value of $73 million.

5. At the height of the Cold War the CIA spent thousands of dollars on a covert operation which involved the theft of a specimen of urine, passed by a member of the Politburo, from a laboratory in Vienna. The CIA regarded it as a great coup. They deduced from the sample, incorrectly as it turned out, that the Russian was seriously ill with kidney disease and didn't have long to live.

6. In 1989 thieves made off with £6,000 worth of frozen bull semen from a university in California. In spite of a £1,000 reward, it was never recovered.

7. In August 1994 Robert Carruthers, 33 years old and homeless, spent the night in a Brighton shop

doorway and woke to find that thieves had stolen his false right leg.

8. A severe national toilet paper shortage in Cuba in 1994 led to the ransacking of a library, where rare books were stolen and torn apart. An official explained that most Cubans had long since used up their telephone books and old magazines.

9. In 1994 Dutch newspapers reported that 10 people in Alphen Aan de Rijn had fallen victim to a denture thief. A telephone caller would persuade victims to leave their dentures in a bag outside the door at night to be collected, refurbished and returned the next morning.

10. In addition to the 1,200 pairs of shoes that the Philippine government confiscated from Imelda Marcos, they also swiped her only bulletproof bra.

10 Strange Discoveries

~

1. During a drugs raid on a house party in Kansas in 1994 police officers found a mummified female head in a box marked "Eight-Piece Party Cook Kit." The head was wrapped in a white lab smock, had blond hair and eyebrows, and its brain had been removed. The owner, 51-year-old Donald Donohue, said that it had been a gift from a medical student.

2. In 1994 police in Nairobi, Kenya, discovered 600 human heads in an abandoned warehouse. It was their first major break since discovering 600 decapitated bodies two years earlier.

3. In November 1994 a Cardiff ice hockey team on a visit to Minsk complained about the smell in the local hotel restaurant. Management later discovered a corpse under the floor.

4. Police and paramedics sparked off an emergency dash across New York City in 1994 after the apparent discovery of a three-month-old human

foetus in a paper bag in the ladies' lavatory of Macy's department store. A police spokesman later revealed that a more detailed medical examination had revealed the contents of the bag to be spaghetti in red sauce.

5. The body of an elderly Swedish woman who died in 1990 lay undiscovered in her Stockholm apartment for more than three years while computers received her pension and automatically paid her bills. The woman's last opened mail was dated 11 May 1990, indicating that she had died at the age of 72.

6. The world record for an undetected death in the home is seven years. In April 1996, 54-year-old Gabriella Villa was discovered in Monza, Italy, seven years after her death by natural causes. Neighbors said they assumed that she had simply moved house.

7. In Sweden in 1994 a man with impaired hearing made a complete recovery after doctors removed a 47-year-old bus ticket from his ear.

8. Genuine items deposited in London Transport's Lost Property Office include a box of false eyeballs, an urn containing the ashes of a recently cremated male, a stuffed bird, a false leg, a bottle of prize bull sperm, half a theatrical prop coffin, a stolen park bench, and a box containing a pair of breast implants.

9. In 1994 the US Ripley's Believe It or Not! museums staged a contest to find the world's largest hairball. The winning hairball, from over 300 entries, was 33 inches in circumference. Sadly, Ripley's subsequently discovered that the Finney County Historical Society Museum in Garden City, Kansas, had upstaged them by discovering a hairball measuring 37 inches.

10. When Richard Ramirez, the notorious US mass murderer known as "Night Stalker," failed a metal detector test at San Francisco County Jail, X-rays detected a variety of items in his rectum, including a small handcuff key, an empty syringe, the cap of a pen, and a small piece of cellophane on which was printed the words "I like chocolate."

10 Firsts

1. Buzz Aldrin was the first man to defecate on the moon.

2. Ronald Reagan was the first president to have his nasal polyps discussed on live TV.

3. On 1 July 1966 Mao Tse-Tung became the first senile septuagenarian to claim a world swimming record. The 72-year-old Chinese leader was reported to have smashed the existing record when he swam 10 miles of the River Yangtze in under an hour. His doctor now thinks it safe to point out that as Mao was too fat to sink or swim, the only way he might have completed even part of the journey (which is highly unlikely) was to have been swept along by the strong river current, unable to get out.

4. George Bush was the first president to be seen throwing up on live TV.

5. Theatre critic Kenneth Tynan became the first man to use the F-word on British television on 13 November 1965. It caused howls of outrage across the country and even in the House of Commons, where prime minister Harold Wilson was obliged to pass comment.

6. Shakespeare was the first writer to use the word "bog."

7. Before he became the first to lose his head, Louis XVI was also the first French king to use a knife and fork, take a regular bath and brush his teeth.

8. The first toilet paper, manufactured in the 1850s, was an unmentionable item, euphemistically referred to by the Victorian advertising profession as "curl papers for hairdressing." Britain's first soft toilet paper, which appeared in 1947, was available only from Harrods.

9. The first frontal lobotomy was experienced by the US quarryman Phineas Gage in 1848. After a quarry explosion, Gage was left with a three-foot crowbar sticking out of his forehead.

Although a doctor was able to put his fingers inside Gage's skull, the quarryman regained consciousness in minutes and lived on for another 12 years. The only noted long-term effect was a marked change in his personality.

10. The first man to design and make a parachute was the Frenchman Louis Sebastian Lenormand, in the late eighteenth century. He did not test it himself: he preferred to drop domestic animals from the the top of the tower of Montpelier Observatory.

10 Former Occupations

1. Genghis Khan: goatherd.

2. Nostradamus: wrote about jam-making.

3. Al Capone: used furniture dealer.

4. Josef Goebbels: accountant.

5. Heinrich Himmler: clerk in an agricultural fertilizer company.

6. Vladimir Ilyich Ulyanov (Lenin): lawyer.

7. Iosif Vissarionovich Dzhugashvili (Joe Stalin): trainee priest.

8. Ronnie and Reggie Kray: agents for Alvin Stardust.

9. Pol Pot: Buddhist monk.

10. US president Gerald R. Ford: male model.

10 Lavatorial Euphemisms

1. Jakes (England, sixteenth century).

2. Necessary house (England, seventeenth century).

3. Cackatorium (England, eighteenth century).

4. Boghouse (England, nineteenth century).

5. Dunny, diddy, toot, brasco (Australia, twentieth century).

6. *Bagno* ("bath"), *cabinetto* ("cabinet") (Italy, twentieth century).

7. *Ubornaya* ("adornment place") (Russia, twentieth century).

8. *Abort* ("away place"), *stlles örtchen* ("silent little place"), *donnerbalken* ("thunder board"), *plumsklo* ("plop closet") (Germany, twentieth century).

9. *Pissoir* (France, twentieth century).

10. *Bestekamer* ("best room") (Holland, twentieth century).

10 Occupational Hazards

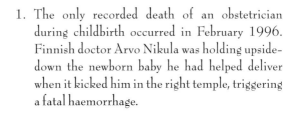

1. The only recorded death of an obstetrician during childbirth occurred in February 1996. Finnish doctor Arvo Nikula was holding upside-down the newborn baby he had helped deliver when it kicked him in the right temple, triggering a fatal haemorrhage.

2. Swedish medical research teams claim to have established that office workers risk damaging their health by inhaling the noxious fumes emitted by their flatulent colleagues – i.e. passive farting. High concentrations of human methane can lead to a variety of serious health problems, including heart disease and serious respiratory problems.

3. The US author Gavin Whitsett was mugged and badly beaten in Evansville, Indiana, in 1994. He is chiefly known for a surprise bestseller which urges his fellow Americans to indulge in random and spontaneous acts of kindness.

4. In May 1994 a French clown called Yves Abouchar died during his circus act, the first clown ever to have choked to death while receiving a custard pie in the face.

5. In 1994 French policeman Pierre Lemieux lost the sight in his right eye after a motorist accidentally spat a peanut into it. Jacques LeMans, who told Paris magistrates that he had his mouth full when he was stopped for speeding and questioned by officer Lemieux, explained: "I just wanted to clear my mouth so I could speak respectfully."

6. From 1956 to 1963 between a quarter and half a million US military personnel were deliberately exposed to fallout from atomic test bombs, mostly without any form of protective clothing or equipment, "for troop training purposes." The US Air Force Brigadier General A.R. Leudecke even complained because his men weren't allowed to stand close enough to the blast.

7. When a team of palace surgeons failed to restore the eyesight of Bohemia's blind King John, he had them all drowned in the Danube.

8. In 1994 a 24-year-old Pakistani textile worker, Ahmed Bulwarj, was knitted to death when he fell head-first into a factory machine used to make cotton fabric. Before his body could be retrieved it had been punctured many hundreds of times by moving knitting needles.

9. Anesthesia by nitrous oxide – "laughing gas" – was discovered in 1884 by Horace Wells, a young dentist living in Connecticut. Wells didn't live long enough to enjoy the full rewards of his marvelous discovery. He became a hopeless chloroform junkie, and one day while high on the drug he ran into the street and doused two passing prostitutes with acid. Wells killed himself before his case came to trial.

10. In April 1983 Mike Stewart, president of the Auto Convoy Company, Dallas, Texas, was standing on the back of a flatbed truck when it passed under a low-level bridge, killing him instantly. At the time he was presenting a piece to camera for a TV item about the dangers of low-level bridges.

10 Rules of Etiquette

1. It is traditional for Russian cosmonauts to urinate on a tyre of the bus that takes them to the launch pad, a custom initiated by Yuri Gagarin himself.

2. According to British royal etiquette, any man suffering from ringworm is exempt from the rule which obliges all men to remove their hats in the presence of the monarch.

3. In Nepal, Narikot wives are obliged to wash their husbands' feet, then drink the dirty water as a token of their devotion.

4. The typical greeting of Masai tribesmen is to spit at each other.

5. In sixteenth-century England it was customary for men to greet female guests by fondling their breasts, provided they were related.

6. According to ancient Jewish law, bad breath is grounds for divorce.

7. Fijian cannibals usually ate with their hands, but as a token of respect for the dead they used a ritual wooden fork for eating people.

8. In accordance with the ancient Indian laws of Manu, any citizen who broke wind in front of the monarch was liable to have his posterior amputated.

9. In some Latin and Mediterranean countries, loud public belching is a sign of appreciation after a good meal.

10. Tibetans used to grow the fingernail long on the little finger of the left hand, so that they could use it to pick their ears and noses clean.

10 Ingenious uses for Ordure

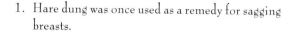

1. Hare dung was once used as a remedy for sagging breasts.

2. Some of the most sought-after varieties of Virginian tobacco got their flavor by being left to cure in lavatories to absorb the fumes of human ordure and urine.

3. A garden centre in Norwalk, California, sells garden gnomes manufactured from recycled cow dung.

4. Class-conscious German farmers traditionally stacked piles of faeces, animal and human, in front of their farms and dwellings. The size of the pile was their way of showing off to the neighbors that they had loads of livestock and could afford a big family.

5. Visitors to the 1994 Winter Olympics were offered souvenir earrings made from elk droppings at £7 a pair.

6. Camel dung was once rubbed into the scalp to make the hair wavy. Ass or hen dung was used to cure skin blemishes, swellings or burns.

7. Cakes of animal excrement, especially pig manure, which contains ammonia, was commonly used in some parts of Britain as an alternative to soap right up until World War II. Women became so immune to the stench of dung on wash days that when soap became popular they often complained that the suds made them nauseous.

8. For centuries most poor people in Britain used cow or horse dung as fuel: although the smell was incredibly offensive, it was free, easy to collect, simple to burn and gave out a great deal of heat. When coal became more easily available in the

late eighteenth and early nineteenth centuries, dung fuel became less common, but the practice continued in Cornwall. On the Isle of Arran, off the west coast of Scotland, it was still the main source of heat in the 1930s.

9. A fashionable salad in eighteenth-century Britain comprised horse dung with mustard and cress.

10. The Alabama mail order company Endangered Faeces sells paperweights made from coprolites – fossilized dinosaur droppings. Each of the 65 million-year-old four-ounce turds is certified as authentic by their own geologist, and each comes with a signed and numbered certificate of authenticity at $60 apiece.

10 Obscure Statistics

~

1. Britain has an estimated three-quarters of a million bedwetters.

2. An estimated 600,000 Americans are impotent from injuries to their crotches. Approximately 40 per cent of these are bicycling accidents.

3. According to a recent survey, one in three male motorists picks his nose while driving.

4. Every day 356,000 people are newly infected with a sexually transmitted disease.

5. India and Bangladesh have exported more human skeletons for medical research than any other countries. The trade is now prohibited as an affront to national dignity.

6. More than 35,000 Americans have had themselves insured against being kidnapped or eaten alive by aliens.

7. On average every glass of London tap water has already passed through the bladders of nine other people.

8. Neither horses nor rabbits can vomit.

9. Impotence is legal grounds for divorce in 24 American states.

10. Irish men suffer less from dandruff than those in any other European country.

10 Litigious People

1. In 1994 Bernadette French, a 36-year-old manic depressive, successfully sued the Wilmington Hospital in Delaware, US, for $1.1 million. A judge ruled that hospital staff had been negligent in allowing her to gouge her own eyes out.

2. A 54-year-old truck driver filed a $10 million lawsuit in Gallatin, Tennessee in April 1996 after he received a defective penile implant. The complainant said he suffered blisters, bruising, infection and embarrassment. His attorney added: "He could be just walking down the street, and it would erect on its own."

3. Robert Jones of Berkshire filed an insurance claim in 1994 against an electricity company for the loss of his parrot. The recently deceased Polly, killed by Jones's dog, had been kept in the family freezer for posterity, but during a power cut had thawed and decomposed.

4. In 1994 a jilted Spaniard broke into his ex-girlfriend's car in Barcelona and blew his brains out with a gun. Vehicle-owner Maria Valdez later sued his family for ruining the interior of her car.

5. Thirty-two-year-old Ernesto Mota suffered brain damage when he swallowed the entire contents of a bag of cocaine in a Chicago police station, so that it could not be used against him as evidence. He sued for the police for $7 million damages because they failed to stop him from doing it.

6. In Albuquerque, New Mexico, George Diesel and his wife sued both Foley's department store and the Levi Strauss Company. According to Mr Diesel, as he was pulling on his Levi 501s for the very first time a faulty fly button rivet tore into his penis, causing him severe pain. Mrs Diesel also sued for the loss of her husband's services.

7. In 1993 Ohio prison inmates Pau Goist and Craig Anthony filed a lawsuit against the company General Foods. They complained that

the company failed to tell them that Maxwell House coffee is addictive, and demanded compensation for the headaches and insomnia they suffered in prison.

8. Vicki Daily of Jackson, Wyoming filed a lawsuit in July 1993 against the widow of the man she had earlier run over and killed in her pick-up truck. Ms Daily demanded compensation from the widow for the "grave and crippling psychological injuries" she suffered while watching the 56-year-old man die.

9. In December 1993 a New York appeals court rejected housewife Edna Hobbs's lawsuit against a company that sold a time-saving kitchen device called The Clapper. The complainant said that in order to turn her appliances on, she clapped until her hands bled. The judge found that Mrs Hobbs had merely failed to adjust the sensitivity controls.

10. In 1994 a handicapped French woman, Yvette LeMons, sued the owner of her rented Toulouse flat for $25,000. Lawyers acting for Miss

LeMons said the apartment owner had allowed termites to enter the premises, which had then eaten her wooden leg, causing her to fall down and break her arm.